Working With and Evaluating
DIFFICULT
SCHOOL
EMPLOYEES

D1605047

Working With and Evaluating

DIFFICULT
SCHOOL
EMPLOYEES

JOHN F. ELLER
SHEILA ELLER

CORWIN
A SAGE Company

For information:

 Corwin
A SAGE Company
2455 Teller Road
Thousand Oaks, California 91320
(800) 233-9936
Fax: (800) 417-2466
www.corwinpress.com

SAGE Ltd.
1 Oliver's Yard
55 City Road
London EC1Y 1SP
United Kingdom

SAGE India Pvt. Ltd.
B 1/I 1 Mohan Cooperative Industrial Area
Mathura Road, New Delhi 110 044
India

SAGE Asia-Pacific Pte. Ltd.
33 Pekin Street #02-01
Far East Square
Singapore 048763

Printed in the United States of America

Library of Congress Cataloging-in-Publication Data

Eller, John, 1957–
Working with and evaluating difficult school employees/John F. Eller and Sheila Eller.
    p. cm.
Includes bibliographical references and index.
ISBN 978-1-4129-5867-7 (cloth : alk. paper)
ISBN 978-1-4129-5868-4 (pbk. : alk. paper)
    1. School personnel management. 2. School employees—Rating of. 3. Problem employees. I. Eller, Sheila. II. Title.

LB2831.5.E39 2010
371.2'01—dc22   2009037004

This book is printed on acid-free paper.

09   10   11   12   13   10   9   8   7   6   5   4   3   2   1

Acquisitions Editor:	Hudson Perigo
Associate Editor:	Julie McNall
Editorial Assistant:	Brett Ory
Production Editor:	Cassandra Margaret Seibel
Copy Editor:	Sarah J. Duffy
Typesetter:	C&M Digitals (P) Ltd.
Proofreader:	Christina West
Indexer:	Jean Casalegno
Cover Designer:	Scott Van Atta

Contents

Preface

We've heard many of our colleagues comment over the years, "My job as a principal would be great if I didn't have to deal with all of those problem people." In spite of increased accountability, trying to help all students be successful, working with a shrinking budget, and making the best of aging facilities, today's principal has to effectively manage and work with the entire staff in order to increase their productivity. In that larger mix comes the ability to work with "difficult" employees.

Just what is a difficult employee? There are as many types of difficult employees as there are employees, but these are generally the people in your school who concern you and cause you to wake up in the middle of the night worrying about them, wondering if you've done enough to work with them to help make them productive members of your staff. These are the employees with the bad attitudes, the ones who are always negative, who seem to cause most of the problems at the school, and who get the most complaints. A difficult employee can cause all kinds of issues and problems for you as the school leader. Each of us has our own definition of difficult employees and the level of difficulty they bring to the job.

Many of us in leadership positions were not like these difficult employees when we were in their positions. Many of us towed the line and tried to do our best. We aspired to be leaders, so we put ourselves in their positions and tried not to cause trouble. As you assumed your first leadership position, you were probably surprised at how many issues some people bring to the workplace. One of the statements we make to the people we work with to improve their skills in working with difficult people is "You will be amazed at all of the creative ways people get into trouble. You will see people do things that get them into trouble that you could have thought of when you were in their position." While this high level of creativity is interesting and, upon reflection, somewhat entertaining, it can be serious and can threaten your school if not addressed properly.

This book was designed to help educational leaders such as principals, assistant principals, superintendents, directors, and other supervisors to learn and apply the techniques and strategies needed in order to effectively deal with difficult school employees. The ideas presented in this book represent not only our knowledge from many different sources over the years but also our own experiences in working with difficult school employees in our various educational roles. We have both had extensive experiences in working productively with marginal, deficient, and downright difficult school employees. As you review the ideas and strategies presented here, you might think our success is due to the fact that we are just confident and "hard" administrators. But we assure you, none of what has made us successful has come naturally; we have had to learn these strategies and fit them into our personalities and leadership styles.

Why is it important that you understand that we are not naturally mean and assertive supervisors? We believe the skills outlined in this book can be learned and implemented by almost anyone or any personality in a leadership position. So whether you are naturally good at conflict and confrontation or you are someone who shies away from negative interactions with others, you can improve your leadership skills and competencies by learning and mastering the skills and strategies that we outline here.

The book is laid out in a manner that we think will benefit you and your understanding as you learn the skills. It is not designed to be read cover to cover, but rather used as a resource where you can go to the specific section that you think will be most beneficial to your own learning. We also tried to keep the information fairly focused on the core you would need in order to understand the concepts presented without providing too much to bog you down in your reading. You will quickly notice the extensive use of templates, bullet points, and key points to help focus your reading. Each chapter begins with a short overview of the content to be presented and ends with a summary and questions to give you a chance to reflect on what you learned as a result of reading.

You will also notice the use of stories and vignettes, all of which are real. Either we have experienced them or colleagues we have worked with over the years have experienced them. To protect the anonymity of those involved, we have changed the names, genders, and situations in presenting these stories and vignettes. We chose to include them in order to provide clear illustrations and ideas for the busy educational leaders using this book.

The book is divided into two distinct sections. The first part, which encompasses Chapters 1–4, outlines some generic strategies and techniques that are intended to be used with difficult school employees. The information provided in Chapter 1, "The Nature of Difficult/Marginal Employees: Why Don't These People Listen to Reason and Improve?" is important because knowing it may help you understand how they got to be difficult and thus develop strategies to work with their situation. Chapter 2, "What Skills and Tools Do I Need in Order to Take On This Situation?" outlines the background you need in order to be successful in working with difficult employees. Chapter 3, "Strategies for Confronting

Marginal and Deficient Behaviors," discusses specific techniques that will help you successfully confront and address the behaviors of the difficult employees that you encounter. One skill normally not developed in school leaders is self-protection. When we choose to take on difficult school employees and deal with their behavior, we place ourselves in a position in which we can become emotionally vulnerable. Chapter 4, "Protecting Yourself When Dealing With Difficult Employees," presents strategies to help you stave off emotionally draining attacks while staying on track with your improvement agenda.

The second part of the book provides specific information for several employee groups that you will most commonly encounter as a school leader. Chapter 5 is titled "Strategies for Working With Difficult/Marginal Teachers." We start with this group because teachers comprise the largest employee group in most schools. Chapter 6, "Strategies for Working With Difficult/Marginal Administrative Assistants and Office Staff," discusses techniques for working positively with these crucial employees. Even though they don't normally have a lot of interactions with children, these employees do interact with parents and members of the public. A difficult or marginal administrative assistant or other office staff member can quickly destroy the climate and reputation of the school.

Finally, two other employee groups are discussed in this text. Chapter 7, "Strategies for Working With Difficult/Marginal Paraprofessionals and Teaching Assistants," focuses on employees that have extended opportunities to interact with children. Schools are hiring more of these professionals as a result of special needs students and declining budgets. Members of this employee group pose unique challenges for school leaders because of their quasiteaching responsibilities coupled with, in many cases, their lack of professional training in teaching techniques. Chapter 8, "Strategies for Working With Difficult/Marginal Custodians," provides ideas for confronting employees in this group. Like office staff, custodians influence parental and public perceptions of your school. Making sure they are competent and working to their fullest potential is paramount to your success as a school leader.

Taking on difficult employees is one of the most difficult parts of our job as school leaders. It is not a part of the job that comes easy. We hope you find the ideas and strategies presented in this book helpful as you take on this challenging but necessary leadership task. We wish you success in this endeavor.

About the Authors

John F. Eller has had a variety of experiences in working with adults over the years that he has been in education. These include working with educational leaders at Virginia Tech University; developing teacher leaders in a master's program; serving as the executive director of Minnesota Association for Supervision and Curriculum Development (ASCD); working as the director of a principal's training center; working as an assistant superintendent for curriculum, learning, and staff development; and serving as principal in a variety of settings. In addition to training and supporting facilitators, John also works in the areas of dealing with difficult people; professional learning communities; employee evaluation; conferencing, coaching, and supervisory skills; strategic planning strategies; school improvement planning and implementation; differentiated instruction; leadership for differentiation; employee recruitment, selection, and induction; and effective teaching strategies.

John has a doctorate in educational leadership and policy studies from Loyola University Chicago and a master's degree in educational leadership from the University of Nebraska at Omaha. He has written books on substitute teaching as well as *The Principal's Guide to Custodial Supervision* and *Effective Group Facilitation in Education: How to Energize Meetings and Manage Difficult Groups*, and he developed the Training Video Series for the Professional School Bus Driver. He has also cowritten *So Now You're the Superintendent!*, the best-selling *Energizing Staff Meetings*, and *Creative Strategies to Transform School Culture*, all published by Corwin.

Sheila Eller has worked in a multitude of educational settings during her career. In addition to her current position as a principal in the Fairfax County (Virginia) Public Schools, she has served as a middle school principal in the Moundsview (Minnesota) School District, a principal in other schools in Minnesota and Illinois, a university professor, a special education teacher, a Title I math teacher, and a self-contained classroom teacher in Grades 1–4. Sheila has also been a member of the executive board of Minnesota ASCD and a regional president of the Minnesota Association of Elementary School Principals. She completed advanced coursework in educational administration and supervision at St. Cloud State University and received a master's degree from Creighton University in Omaha, Nebraska, and a bachelor's degree from Iowa State University.

Sheila is a regular presenter at the national conventions of the Association for Supervision and Curriculum Development, sharing her expertise on the topic of effective staff meetings and multiage instruction. While she served as a professor at National-Louis University in Evanston, Illinois, she worked on the development team for a classroom mathematics series that was adopted by several districts in the region; her classroom and instructional techniques were featured on a video that was produced as a complement to this series. She works with educators in developing energized staff meetings, school improvement initiatives, multiage teaching strategies, employee supervision, and other teaching and learning content areas. Sheila has coauthored the best-selling *Energizing Staff Meetings* and *Creative Strategies to Transform School Culture*, both published by Corwin.

1

The Nature of
Difficult/Marginal
Employees

*Why Don't These People Listen
to Reason and Improve?*

In many schools across the country, there are a variety of challenges facing principals. You may have had training or coursework on working
with the curriculum, understanding data and assessment information, and
processing other information related to the structural components of a
school, but you have probably received minimal support in dealing with
the human elements of a school. These human elements can be complicated
and complex to deal with effectively. An area of difficulty for principals and
other school leaders involves working with employees who are not performing up to standards and need to make changes. In many instances,
these people require much work and focus in order to improve. From our
experiences working with these employees, it is important to understand
the background of their behaviors and put together a comprehensive plan
(including follow-up) for addressing their behaviors. In this chapter, you
will begin your journey toward getting a handle on the issues presented by

1

these employees by understanding the foundation or background of their behaviors. In this chapter you will learn about the following:

- identifying negative employees' frames of reference
- the characteristics of difficult employees
- how to respond to change
- the possible causes of negative behavior
- faculty responses and contribution to resistance

Understanding the cause or root of the problem is essential to addressing it. Let's see how a relatively new principal works to find out some of the potential causes of her administrative assistant's performance:

It is her third year as the principal of Paul Middle School, and Heather is bothered by the attitude of her administrative assistant, Barb. When Barb talks with parents and answers the phone, she is very curt and short. Several parents have approached Heather about the problem, and even the Parent Teacher Organization president has mentioned it. Heather has decided to try to improve the situation. In doing some investigational work, she has found that this behavior has been going on for at least 5 years, the entire time Barb has been at the school. Heather decides to gather some more information about why Barb acts this way before confronting the issue.

Through her discussions with others and with Barb, Heather has found that Barb views parent interactions as interruptions of her normal routine. She said that she feels that some parents have nothing better to do than come into the school and bother her with trivial issues. Barb has told Heather and others that she feels she has a lot of work to do and that these parents are keeping her from completing this work. She gets frustrated and short with them. Now that Heather understands at least a portion of the problem, she is ready to move forward in putting together a plan to deal with the issues of Barb's performance.

As you can see from this example, Heather takes some time to understand the root causes of Barb's performance before formulating a plan and beginning to address the problem. This is one crucial part of addressing the issues presented by employees.

FRAMES OF REFERENCE

In dealing with a variety of employees and problems over the years, we have found that many of them involve a structured frame of reference by the employee in question. In this section, we will examine the basics of this principle and provide ideas for how to identify it and develop strategies and ideas to address the negative situation.

In his groundbreaking book *The Structure of Scientific Revolutions*, Thomas Kuhn (1996) examines the development of scientific discovery and thought. We have adapted his basic structure to identify the stages that people go through in developing their thoughts and patterns related to both their professional and personal behaviors.

FRAMES OF REFERENCE

- A person experiences a series of events. Her mind takes in the information or data from these experiences.
- The person's mind begins to see common attributes from these experiences and the information drawn from them. Her mind starts to put together the information from these situations and draw conclusions about the experiences.
- These conclusions begin to form definite patterns. The patterns work together to become a way of thinking or frame of reference for the person. This frame of reference begins to govern the way she sees the world and becomes reality for her.
- Because of the frame of reference, a comfort zone is established for the person. Experiences and information that fit into this frame of reference reinforce her thought pattern. She becomes comfortable in her existing thought pattern because it establishes predictability for her. Incoming information is filtered through this frame of reference. Information that matches the frame is reinforced; information that is counter to it can be discounted.
- Over time, the living or work environment can change. The person becomes uncomfortable with the new environment because it doesn't fit her frame of reference. To remain comfortable and reinforce the old thought pattern, she may change or discount the information being provided in the new environment.
- Because the person is trying to fit the new information from the environment into an old frame of reference, she can become resistant to the new thought patterns, behaviors, or information coming to her.
- After exposure to the new information or ideas for a period of time, the person begins to see how it connects or is related to her original frame of reference. The new incoming information begins to assist her as she develops a new frame of reference. Over time, she is able to embrace the new ideas and integrate them into her operating procedures.

Source: Adapted from Eller, 2004.

The information about frames of reference is very important because it helps explain why some people are difficult to work with as employees. At times, their ways of thinking about a topic or idea can be shaped by their environments and experiences. Keeping this in mind helps us as supervisors to deal with them and some of their behaviors. When we understand how someone learned a behavior, it can be easier to figure out how to help him learn a new behavior. Understanding another person's perspective is an important part of our success in dealing with negative or difficult employees. We introduce the concept of frames of reference here so you can consider how you will try to understand others and use this information to provide appropriate supervision.

CHARACTERISTICS OF DIFFICULT EMPLOYEES

Unfortunately, human behavior has a lot of variability and some unpredictability. We recognize that every situation is different from another, but we have found some commonalities in the difficult employees we have dealt with in the past. In this section, we will share several of those characteristics and some practical considerations for dealing with them.

Lack of Awareness of Negative Behavior

At times, employees are really not aware of the impact that their behaviors have on others. They move through their jobs (and sometimes their lives) not really being able to see how what they do affects others. This is caused to some extent by the fact that they though life with blinders on or with tunnel vision.

Possible Remedies

As the supervisor, it is crucial for you to provide feedback or information to the employee in order to help her see her unproductive habits. You have to try to figure out the best way to deliver this information in her preferred processing style so that she will see and understand it. For example, if an employee is a structured, data-driven person, you will need to deliver the information in a factual, concrete manner. If the person is relationship oriented, you may need to deliver the information in a manner more closely related to relationships. We'll talk in more detail about specific strategies in later chapters.

Denial of Negative Behavior

Denial of the behavior can be related to the fact that employees are unaware of the problem or do not want to deal with the issue. As the supervisor, you have to decide the motivation behind the denial. Normally, we give offending employees the benefit of the doubt initially. But we quickly move to believing that the denial has a manipulative purpose when employees continue to use the negative behavior after we have identified it. From our experiences, some employees will put more energy into denial than it would have taken them to eliminate the problem in the first place. This could stem from the fact that they have been able to wait out previous supervisors who confronted them about problems.

Possible Remedies

As the supervisor, you need to let the employee know that you mean business when it comes to addressing the negative behavior. You will need to be direct and to the point when talking to him about the situation and be ready to follow up to see if the behavior has improved or if you need to move to the next disciplinary level. Our advice is to make sure you are ready both procedurally and emotionally when you begin to confront an employee about his negative behavior. We will offer more information about specific strategies in later chapters.

Blaming Others for Their Situation or Behavior

This behavior is closely related to denial but has some subtle differences, so it needs to be handled as a separate category. Difficult employees normally have become very good at shifting the blame for their inadequacies to others. Sometimes, they actually believe what they are telling you, but in most cases they use this technique as a form of manipulation to get you off their back.

Possible Remedies

When confronting a marginal or difficult employee, listen for cues that let you know she is trying to set the blame elsewhere. As you hear this happening, use a variety of strategies to address the situation. At times, we have stopped an employee in mid sentence and let her know that we understand what she is attempting to do and that we won't be thrown off track by it. In other cases, we have let the employee finish the statement and then asked focused questions that let her know we won't be fooled by the manipulative technique and that help steer the conversation toward resolution of the problem. In other cases, we listen to the employee's story/excuses and then confront the situation. In any case, you need to let the employee know that shifting of blame will not excuse her behavior and that it needs to be addressed. We will provide specific examples and ideas about how to address this type of behavior in each chapter that deals with specific employee groups.

Justifying Their Behavior Based on the Expectations of a Previous Supervisor

As hard it may seem to believe, this is a common defense we have seen used by employees over the years. Normally, they make comments like "Bill told me . . ." or "The last two principals didn't have a problem with . . ." or "You are the first supervisor to . . ." These kinds of statements related to previous supervisors are meant to undermine your confidence and make you back down on your demands. In our work with principals over the years, this technique has been successfully used by many employees.

Possible Remedies

When an employee uses this technique, you need to recognize the manipulation and take steps to avoid being sucked in. If you begin to doubt your leadership (which is normal, by the way), you allow the employee to take you down the path of letting him off the hook. When he starts to talk about the supervision techniques and priorities of a previous supervisor, you need to respond in a positive but assertive manner. Comments such as "Thank you for your thoughts about (name the topic), but things are different now" or "I am a different supervisor than (name the person) and have some different expectations" let the employee know that you understand his perspective but need to operate the school in the manner that you feel best meets the needs of students under the current conditions. You may want to contact the previous supervisor to let that person know what is happening and that when you make comments about your leadership priorities to the employee you are not trying to make negative comments about the previous supervisor's priorities. Since the employee is trying to undermine your confidence, be sure to let him know, as you confront the issues related to his behavior, that this technique will not work on you.

THE RESPONSE TO CHANGE

People in general can be resistant to change. Difficult employees may dedicate much more effort to resisting change than it would take to learn the new idea or procedure associated with a change. In this section, we'll describe some of the behaviors we have witnessed over the years as we have worked with difficult or angry employees in relation to the change process.

Waiting You Out

In many instances, difficult employees have been in their positions for a number of years. They may have survived other principals who have tried unsuccessfully to deal with their performance issues. These principals may have moved on to other jobs, but the employees have stayed behind. Because of this survival behavior, some of these employees have learned how to mask their deficiencies or resist your directives until you, too, move on to greener pastures.

To combat this phenomenon, you will need to clearly communicate to the employee that you are interested in working with her in the long run. You may need to communicate your seriousness in order to attack her deficits. We have found it beneficial to clearly communicate that you understand the "waiting you out" behavior as well as your seriousness and level of focus related to the employee's issues. As with any effort to deal with deficient performance, building a sound follow-up program to change it is crucial to your success as a principal.

Justifying Why the Existing Behavior Is Much Better Than the New Behavior

Employees exhibiting deficient behaviors sometimes spend a lot of time and energy justifying their deficient behaviors. You have to identify this situation, know it's happening, and help the employee work through the issue. The challenge you will face is to acknowledge the situation without causing the employee to dig in on the issue or to think that you agree with his assessment of the soundness of his antiquated thinking. Here is a process that we use to combat this type of situation:

- Listen to the employee's description of why the old or existing behavior is better for him than the behavior required by the new procedure. Don't confirm or refute his perception at this point in the conversation.
- Ask the employee to provide more specific information to outline or justify his beliefs. Ask him to also provide evidence for his beliefs.
- Outline your ideas for the new procedure. Draw connections between your ideas and the old procedures. Help the employee see the larger outcome rather than the short-term technique or procedure.
- Develop a schedule outlining how the employee will transition to the new procedure. Be sure to identify the follow-up and support that will be provided to assist him in making the transition.
- If the employee is not willing to adopt the new procedure, you need to decide the importance or soundness of the new procedure. If it is sound, you need to work through a more aggressive strategy to implement it. If the resistance is not warranted, you may need to move toward transfer or termination with this employee.

Encouraging Others to Resist Change

At times, employees seek the comfort of others when resisting change. They may think that getting others on the bandwagon will help them feel supported and will effectively resist the change. As a leader, you will need to address this type of issue head-on. Here are some strategies we have found helpful:

- Meet with the individual and try to understand her perspective.
- Talk to the entire group that is participating in or supporting the resistance. Work with them to help them understand the new procedure.

Help them see how it will help further the long-term objectives of the school or organization.

- Talk with members of the resistance group individually or in small groups. Help them understand the new procedure. Help them see the connections between it and their existing practices.

Deliberately Making Mistakes With the New Procedure to Sabotage It

This is a common response to change by people wanting to resist. You have to recognize what is happening and the motivation behind the actions, and develop a strategy to deal with the issue. In many cases, we have found it helpful to make sure that those charged with implementing the new procedure are given the appropriate amount or training and development in order to ensure success. Designing and implementing an effective follow-up plan is also essential to success. We have also found that sitting down and having a heart-to-heart conversation with a sabotaging employee may also improve the situation.

Recruiting Community Members to Pressure You to Abandon the New Procedure

This common strategy to resist change can be very destructive to the operation of the school. Some employees use their community connections and relationships to drum up support for the status quo. This type of behavior is common in medium-sized and smaller communities because employees tend to be closely connected as a result of their longevity at the school and/or live in the community or neighborhood. We have found over the years that taking a direct approach to this type of situation has some merit. First, it's important to talk with the employee about his strategy and how it not only undermines the success of the school and his credibility, but also involves outsiders who have no business being involved in school operations. We normally try to listen to the employee's concern and direct him back to appropriate ways of voicing his opposition within the building or district. At times and with careful thought, we have even had to prevent an employee from involving community members outside of the school in a particular situation.

UNDERSTANDING THE SOURCE OF THE DIFFICULTY

We outlined some of the potential causes of negative employee behavior because it is important for you to take the time to think about why this behavior could be happening. Once you are able to identify the potential causes of the behavior, you may be better able to design a strategy to address the problem. Consider the template provided in Figure 1.1 to help you diagnose the possible causes of your difficult employee's performance or behavior issues.

SUMMARY

In this chapter, we have addressed some of the reasons why people develop the behaviors that make them difficult to work with. It is important that you begin your efforts to confront difficult people by understanding the background experiences that may be contributing to the problem. We have found that approaching people using strategies based on this understanding helps to de-escalate potentially emotionally charged or negative situations. This behavior has worked to our advantage in many cases and we have been able to work through situations without having to do major interventions or terminate staff members.

In putting the foundational aspects outlined in this chapter to work, take a few minutes to reflect on the following:

- Why is it important to try to understand the potential cause(s) of the employee behavior problem before formulating a strategy to address it?
- How does understanding the Frame of Reference model help you gain insight into the problem an employee may be exhibiting?
- What does a difficult employee stand to gain by enlisting the support of others in a resistance effort? How can you as the leader approach this situation?

In the real world, there are people who do not respond to the simple strategies we have outlined in this chapter. For them, you will need to move forward in an aggressive manner. The rest of the chapters in this book will provide you with strategies and ideas to help you be successful in changing their behavior or terminating their employment.

What skills do supervisors need in order to deal with these especially difficult employees? How do supervisors know whether they have the skills needed to work with such employees? How do supervisors who feel they are missing key skills, or want to improve the skills they have, set goals and gradually improve their abilities in this area? In Chapter 2, we will describe some ways to assess your present skill set and develop a sound learning plan to attain the skills you need in order to be successful in working with difficult employees.

Figure 1.1   Difficulty Foundation or Source Diagnostic Template

Use this template as you work to understand the potential source of the difficulty you are experiencing from your employee. Once you have identified the potential source or sources of the difficulty, you will be better equipped to develop and design an intervention plan to diminish the difficulty or move to terminate service.

1. What do you think have been the past experiences of this employee that may have shaped his or her behaviors and attitudes?

_____

_____

2. How do you think this employee has been supervised in the past? What influence might this have in relation to his or her attitude or performance?

_____

_____

3. What pressures outside of the workplace do you think this employee experiences? How might these pressures impact his or her attitude and energy?

_____

_____

4. What age/experience factors do you think influence this employee, and how do those issues play into the situation?

_____

_____

5. What do you think are the employee's preferred tasks and operating styles? Does he or she seem to like to work in isolation or get energy from interacting with others?

_____

_____

6. What have you noticed that seems to motivate this person to do his or her best in the workplace? What do you notice that tends to lower this person's energy or motivation while on the job?

_____

_____

NOTES

Write any notes that you think might be helpful to you as you implement the strategies/ideas presented in this chapter with your difficult employees. Feel free to refer back to these notes as you need to when confronting their issues or behaviors.

_____

_____

_____

_____

_____

_____

_____

_____

_____

_____

_____

_____

_____

_____

_____

_____

_____

2

What Skills and Tools Do I Need in Order to Take On This Situation?

So you have decided to take on a difficult employee or situation. What do you need in order to be successful and survive? While every situation is different and the supervisory needs can vary based on the specifics of the problem, there are some core competencies that help ensure your success in this process. In this chapter, we will examine several of those core competencies, focusing on the following:

- the definition of success when working with difficult or deficient employees
- your skills and readiness in dealing with a difficult situation or person
- understanding and being able to break down the employee's job description and relating the performance issues to this description
- planning a conference related to performance improvement
- personal tools to handle the difficult conversations you will have to hold in order to work with difficult employees

Taking on the responsibility of dealing with a difficult employee can be challenging, but it can work. See how Phil handles one of his custodians in the following example:

Phil, a high school principal, has watched a situation involving one of his custodians, Reggie, unfold over a short period of time. He has concerns about Reggie's performance. Before addressing the situation, Phil thinks it through to prepare himself for the possible confrontation. Through this analysis, he finds that he needs to learn more about how Reggie thinks and the exact details of his job description. He also considers how he will need to explain to Reggie exactly what needs to be improved and how Phil wants him to improve. After doing this analysis, Phil begins to develop a plan for moving forward. When he is ready, he requests a time to meet with Reggie so that he can lay out his concerns and his plan to improve the situation. He approaches the conference with confidence and is able to address the situation in a positive and productive manner.

While the details of exactly what Phil proposed are left out of this story, we can see that the time he put into planning and preparation helped him feel confident and collected as he approached the situation. As you will see, this planning and preparation will be key as you approach the improvement of your staff members.

BACKGROUND OF EMPLOYEE DISCIPLINE

The major focus of this book is practical guidance related to dealing with employees; it is not a legal guide to termination. We advise you to always seek out appropriate legal advice before you begin your actions against a particular employee. If your district retains the services of an attorney, consider talking with this person before addressing an employee. If not, your personnel department of direct supervisor may be able to provide you with the legal assistance you need in order to be successful in confronting deficient employees.

Just Cause

As you begin to think about dealing with difficult employees on your staff, remember that they have legal protection from unwarranted or frivolous actions. You need to make sure that the inappropriate behavior or performance concern is serious enough to warrant action, that is, that you have *just cause* in taking action against them. When there is just cause for addressing a certain behavior, the employee is protected from having to respond to petty or unimportant issues. Your concerns must be based on deficiencies that are directly related to the success of the school.

Due Process

The term *due process* is based in the U.S. Constitution and deals with the rights of employees and the fairness of their treatment by you as their supervisor. In general, when considering due process, you need to do the following:

- Share your concerns about the performance of the employee directly with her.
- Identify the basis for the concern or the person accusing the employee.
- Allow the employee a chance to share her side of the story.
- Make a fair determination of the situation, taking into account all of the information available. You should clearly communicate the results of this decision to the employee.
- If the employee disagrees with you, there are other channels or strategies that can be undertaken to ensure fairness or impartiality related to the issue.

Employee Discipline

In most settings, a hierarchy of discipline is used when working with difficult employees. This is typically called *progressive discipline.* It is progressive in nature because the consequences for initial performance issues or off-task behavior are usually minor but the severity increases as the behavior or frequency of behavior increases. Here is an example of a progressive discipline plan:

- first incident—oral reminder
- second incident—oral reprimand
- third incident—written reprimand
- fourth incident—suspension of employee/investigation
- fifth incident—termination of employee

A COMPETENCIES-BASED APPROACH TO THINKING ABOUT EMPLOYEE PROBLEMS

In preparing to work with difficult staff members, you should take the time to analyze their job requirements and examine the competencies needed to be successful in their job. Here, we look at two types of competencies to consider when approaching performance issues.

Base competencies. These are the kinds of skills that are at the core of an employee's person or personality. They tend to cover more of the affective part of the job. Base competencies cannot be easily taught but must be developed over time with support and coaching. Their absence tends to lead to termination from job assignments. Here are a few examples of base competencies:

- ability to build rapport with others
- ability to listen actively in a conversation
- empathy
- an understanding of surrounding situations ("withitness")
- ability to multitask

Surface competencies. These are the kind of skills that are most directly related to the technical aspects of the job. Surface competencies are the skills typically taught to employees as a part of their job orientation/induction process; they can be learned fairly quickly and measured in a straightforward manner. Deficits in surface competencies can lead to termination for inefficiency or incompetence in job performance. Here are a few examples of these competencies:

- ability to use word-processing skills to complete tasks
- ability to operate cleaning equipment
- ability to complete required reports
- ability to administer tests and assessments
- ability to operate a computer and the software necessary to complete required job tasks

Figure 2.1 provides a template for assessing base and surface competencies, and Figure 2.2 includes a sample of a completed template.

THE DEFINITION OF SUCCESS WHEN WORKING WITH DIFFICULT OR DEFICIENT EMPLOYEES

You will need to define your expected level of success when confronting the performance of deficient or difficult employees. Sometimes, you will be able to completely change the employee and get his behavior and performance on track. In other instances, you may see a slight change in behavior or performance. In many instances, however, you will not see any changes in behavior or performance. Here are some questions to consider:

- How do you decide if the employee will be able to change or improve performance?

  We have found that it is much easier to help an employee refine a deficit in surface competencies than in base competencies. If you are working with an employee that has to improve only a few surface competencies, she has a fairly good chance of improving. On the other hand, an employee that has a deficit in several base competencies may need extensive work to improve them. Since base competencies develop over time with support, the employee may not be able to improve her skills in an appropriate amount of time with reasonable effort.

Figure 2.1   Template for Plotting Base and Surface Competencies

Use this template to assess your employees' skills and classify them as foundational (base) or technical (surface). Completing this template will help you as you begin to assess their needs and develop strategies to deal with the issues they present. Listing and classifying the skills will help you determine the level of difficulty in improving employees' performance or moving toward termination.

Name _____   Job or Position _____

Job Requirement/ Competency	Base Competency	Surface Competency	Deficit Skill

Figure 2.2	Sample Completed Base and Surface Competencies Template

This is a sample template to assist you as you begin to assess your difficult employees and develop strategies to improve their performance or move toward termination.

Name <u>Jane Doe</u>   Job or Position <u>Administrative Assistant</u>

Job Requirement/ Competency	Base Competency	Surface Competency	Deficit Skill
Meeting and greeting visitors to the school	X		X
Typing reports		X	
Balancing the school budget		X	
Assisting new parents with paperwork	X		X
Scheduling appointments for the principal		X	X
Answering the phone in a friendly/ helpful manner	X		X
Advising the principal about interpersonal needs at the school	X		X
Organizing the office space for efficient operation		X	

- What amount of growth and change should you reasonably expect?

  Once you understand the issues impacting the performance of an employee and help to eliminate then, you should expect that he can make the kind of improvements that will enable him perform his job at an appropriate level within a few weeks. The appropriate level of performance is something that you should determine based on his level of experience, the complexity of the work required, the amount of support provided to him, and so on. Any of these factors will slow the employee's growth if not coordinated and managed during the improvement process.

- How bad does someone need to be before you intervene?

  We have found that several factors impact the decision to intervene and address an employee's performance. Look at the impact on the school or organization. If the person's behavior is negatively impacting students, it's time to move in. Also, if others in her division are noticing the problem and the negative behavior is impacting the quality of her work, you need to intervene.

- What is a reasonable amount of growth to expect from an employee?

  The expected progress can be hard to gauge. You need to look at where the employee started and see how far he needs to go in order to move forward. Once you have clarified the expectations, he should be able to make improvements at about the same pace you would expect from an employee relatively new to the workplace. For example, in working with a new custodial employee, you would expect that after two to three nights of orientation he should be able to complete his assigned section with minimal supervision. Of course, you wouldn't expect this new custodian to understand the intricacies of the job in this short amount of time, just be able to follow an established schedule.

- When do you decide that enough is enough?

  After you have invested the appropriate amount of time and attention in an employee, if you have not seen the kind of growth that you would reasonably expect, it's probably time to consider moving toward termination. Be sure that you have documented your efforts in helping her to grow and change so that, as you move forward in the termination process, you will be working from a firm foundation.

YOUR READINESS IN DEALING WITH A DIFFICULT SITUATION OR PERSON

We have discovered that difficult employees can be strong in their convictions. When getting ready to take on a difficult employee or situation, you need to be well prepared. It has been our experience that some of these people will bring a lot of resistance and power sources to bear in order to maintain the status quo. If you underestimate the amount of power these employees have or the lengths they will go to fight you, you could be surprised and defeated almost as soon as you get started. In confronting problematic behavior, we have found the following core set of skills to be especially helpful in our own experiences and in the work we have done to support others when they have chosen to take on these battles.

An Understanding of the Employee's Job Description or Performance Expectations

Be sure to take the time to review and get to know the job descriptions, schedules, and performance expectations of your employee groups. When you know the details of these documents, you will be better able understand the job responsibilities of your staff members. You can use this information as an assessment to help you determine whether a staff member is off track or on track in regard to performance. Figure 2.3 provides a sample assessment template.

Figure 2.3 Employee Improvement Assessment Template

Name _____   Job or Position _____

1. List the deficit skills you are concerned about in relation to this employee.

    Base Competencies _____

    _____

    Surface Competencies _____

    _____

2. List the impact of these deficits.

    Negative Impact on the Organization _____

    _____

    Negative Impact on Individuals _____

    _____

3. How much of your time do you need to invest in this employee to help improve his or her performance?

    _____

    How quickly do you need the performance issues to improve with this employee?

    _____

    Can you and the organization handle the amount of time it will take this employee to improve?

    _____

Ability to Accurately Describe the Deficit in Performance

In beginning to address the performance of an employee, you need to be clear and specific. Unless you can be clear and specific in your assessment and targeting of employee performance, you have no business in addressing concerns. Having clarity not only helps you specifically target the inappropriate behavior but increases your credibility as a supervisor. If you have a "feeling" that there is something wrong in the work environment but can't quite put your finger on it, take the time to investigate or gather more data until you are able to be clear and direct.

Ability to Confront the Employee About Performance

It takes a lot of courage to confront people about their job performance. We all get a little nervous when thinking about the confrontation process, but we need to muster the strength and courage to follow through and complete the process. It is possible to do this in a number of ways:

- Identify that the problem you are confronting is the employee's, not yours. Your job is to make the person aware of the situation and work to improve it for the employee and the school.
- Identify what normally makes you uncomfortable when confronting employee problems. Think through how you can get through those uncomfortable moments to actually improve the situation.
- Rehearse your potentially confrontational conversation with a colleague in advance of meeting with the employee.
- Practice delivering the potentially confrontational message by recording it on a tape recorder and then listening to it. As it plays back, listen for statements that may cause a reaction on the part of the employee; be sure to refine any unnecessary reactionary statements.
- Think through the worst-case scenario related to the employee's reaction to the negative message; determine your strategies for handling the reactions.
- Think through how to deliver the message quickly and efficiently. Make sure that you get the point across without adding in a lot of extra words.
- Use visuals to assist in the delivery of the message. Place the visuals between you and the employee so they reinforce the message you are trying to deliver.
- Ask for the presence of a colleague during the difficult message as a witness and to provide support.
- Think through the temporary discomfort associated with the confrontation and compare it to the discomfort felt every day as the employee continues to repeat the irritating behavior.
- Set up the potentially negative meeting for the end of the week or right before an extended break so you will not have to interact with the employee right after the confrontation.

Ability to Design a Difficult Conference With the Employee

A great amount of the success experienced by supervisors when addressing their concerns with an employee's performance stems from their ability to plan and deliver an effective conference with the employee. When a growth conference is well thought out and planned, it takes the ambiguity out of the conversation and provides needed clarity for the employee. Because of the emotions associated with employee deficiencies and the seriousness of the issues you are planning to address, this is no time to be "winging it" in your performance as a supervisor. When we first coach people on this skill, we provide an outline for them to follow in planning their conference. We also advise them to bring a copy of their plan/outline to the actual conference and refer to it as needed during the interaction. In these kinds of situations, your emotions could work to diminish your thought process, which could make you forget or misplace your ideas. If you have a written plan nearby, you will be able to refer to it from time to time to stay on track.

Here are some of the components that are helpful to include in a written plan to confront employee deficiencies:

- your opening statements to start the meeting or difficult conversation
- a general statement outlining the areas where you have concerns with this employee's performance
- specific examples that illustrate the deficient performance you want to address, including exactly what you have seen that has led you to the conclusion that there is a deficient performance and the specific dates and any previous discussions you had with the employee related to the issues you are planning to address n this conference
- the exact language you will use to state that the issues you have identified are deficient or not meeting district standards, including specific language related to why you think these deficiencies are harmful to others or the organization
- clear and focused directives for eliminating or refining the identified areas of deficiency, which clearly state your desire and expectations for the employee to improve
- an outline of a plan for you to work with the employee and conduct follow-up in order to make sure the issues you identified are addressed and improved; in the conference, you should identify dates for checkups and further communication between you and the employee
- a statement that you expect these issues to be addressed in a timely manner, perhaps letting the employee know that consequences will follow if the deficits are not addressed and eliminated in a reasonable timeframe
- statements that you will use to close the meeting, assess the employee's understanding of the situation, and confirm the plan developed during the conference

Skill in Addressing the Issue While Staying on Track

During a meeting like this, some employees will do whatever they need to take you off track. If they can get you off track, they can avoid accountability for their actions and continue with business as usual. Be sure that you have strategies in place to identify when someone is trying to take you off track and how to refocus the conversation in order to get back on track. Over the years we have used many good techniques, including the following, to get and keep conversations on track:

- Use a framing statement at the beginning of a conference to lay out the parameters of the conversation. A framing statement draws a verbal boundary around a conversation and holds it together. We will share more details about framing later, but you generally want to deliver a statement that keeps the other person on track, for example, "Today we are here to focus on the issues I have with your job performance." That statement clearly outlines the focus of the meeting. When the employee starts to get off track by bringing up other unrelated issues, you can say, "We aren't talking about (the off-track topic) today, we need to stay focused on the issues with your performance."

- Recognize when the employee is trying to bring up an unrelated issue to take you off track, and squelch discussion of that topic. When the employee brings up the off-track issue, you need to quickly recognize it and discount it. For example, in a recent conference, an employee said, "The reason I am having trouble is because you gave me the worst students." The supervisor quickly recognized the off-track technique and said, "I randomly assigned the sections. All the classes have a similar makeup. My issues with your performance revolve around how you react to situations that happen in your classroom." This statement disempowered the employee's effort to take the supervisor off-track and kept the conference focused.

- Use gesturing to bring the employee back to core of the conversation. When the employee is going off on a tangent, hold up a stop gesture (hand held out in front, palm toward the employee) and tell the person to stop and get back on track.

- Plan statements in your outline or script that you can use to get the employee back on track. In most cases, you know the employee well and can anticipate a potentially off-track comment. Plan out in advance what you will say and how you will deal with this situation so you aren't taken by surprise when it happens in the conference.

Ability to Design and Implement
a Follow-Up Plan for the Employment Plan

If your intent is to first help the employee improve before making any decisions about future employment, you should design an improvement and follow-up plan to ensure growth on the part of the employee. A clear plan ensures that you will provide the employee with the support to succeed. Here are the components of an effective improvement plan:

- a clear statement of the deficient behaviors or work performance issues
- the reasons why the improvements are needed
- the specific behaviors or replacement strategies that the employee needs to implement in order to improve
- the timeline according to which the improvements should be started and fully implemented
- a schedule stating not only when you and the employee will meet again to talk about progress made in relation to the required criteria, but also when you will gather data or observe to assess the growth accomplished by the employee

As you approach the difficult task of confronting an employee, it is a good idea to assess your skills and the degree to which you are ready to address the situation and the employee.

THE USE OF JOB DESCRIPTIONS IN YOUR WORK WITH DIFFICULT SCHOOL EMPLOYEES

When choosing to address negative or deficient employee behaviors, be sure to take the time to look over evaluation criteria or job descriptions. These documents can be helpful because they provide you with the specific details you need in order to confront difficult employees. In examining job descriptions, look for the following:

- clearly defined expectations and behaviors
- general expectations or themes for employee performance indicators, which will provide you with an idea about the scope of the employee's work
- gradations that outline examples of deficient, basic, and exemplary employee performance, which you can use to share what you see as employees' present level of performance and what you expect from them in terms of future performance levels

Always work from the position of extensive knowledge when it comes to addressing employee deficiencies. Since they may have more experience than you in actually doing the work, make sure that you thoroughly understand and can articulate the major components and expectations related to the job. If you haven't taken the time to understand and be able to clearly identify your concerns and expectations, you will put the employees in a power position. You want to be in the power position when dealing with difficult school employees.

SUMMARY

As a supervisor, you need to feel comfortable and confident in working with difficult employees. One way to increase your comfort and confidence is to take a look at your own skills and the deficits of your marginal or difficult employees. Figure 2.4 provides a sample self-assessment template. Beyond just identifying your skills, it's crucial that you take stock in the needs of your employees. Tools and strategies designed to assist you in assessing both your needs and the needs of your employees have been provided in this chapter.

As you finish reading this chapter, think about your response to the following questions:

- How do the concepts of base competencies versus surface competencies impact your work with difficult or marginal employees?
- What are the crucial skills you need to posses as a supervisor in order to be effective in addressing deficit employee skills?
- How can you increase your confidence and competence in working with difficult employees?

In this chapter, we have addressed some of the foundation or basic skills needed to begin the process of confronting a deficient employee. In Chapter 3, we will go much more in depth in outlining specific tools that you can use to improve how you function with difficult employees. As you review the information in Chapter 3, be sure to think through how you might use it when confronting employees from all classifications in the school. Also be sure to picture yourself using the techniques and assess your comfort with doing so. They will work for you as you take on these marginal or deficient employees.

| Figure 2.4 | Readiness Self-Assessment Template |

Confronting employee deficiencies requires a set of sound skills. Use this template to help you assess your skills in this area. Use the results to help you decide how to move forward with your particular situation and to develop a professional growth plan to help you gain the necessary skills to feel competent in moving forward in your work with this employee.

Skill Required to Deal With Employee	Your Level of Skill in This Area (1–10; 1 = Very Limited, 5 = Somewhat Prepared, 10 = Very Prepared)	Evidence for Rating	Strategy or Resource Needed for Addressing Skill Limitation
Ability to accurately describe the deficit in performance	1 2 3 4 5 6 7 8 9 10		
Ability to design a difficult conference with the employee	1 2 3 4 5 6 7 8 9 10		
Ability to confront the employee about performance	1 2 3 4 5 6 7 8 9 10		
Skill in addressing the issue while staying in track	1 2 3 4 5 6 7 8 9 10		
Ability to design an improvement plan	1 2 3 4 5 6 7 8 9 10		
Ability to design and implement a follow-up plan for the employment plan	1 2 3 4 5 6 7 8 9 10		
Ability to work under pressure and stay the course to the final outcome	1 2 3 4 5 6 7 8 9 10		

NOTES

Write any notes that you think might be helpful to you as you implement the strategies/ideas presented in this chapter with your difficult employees. Feel free to refer back to these notes as you need to when confronting their issues or behaviors.

_____

_____

_____

_____

_____

_____

_____

_____

_____

_____

_____

_____

_____

_____

3

Strategies for Confronting Marginal and Deficient Behaviors

❖

Marty, the principal of Washington High School, was concerned about the performance of one of his custodians. Marty suspected that the night supervisor, Bob, was stealing equipment from the school. At various times during the year, the industrial arts room was missing some hand tools. Marty conducted a preliminary investigation and found that Bob was the only night person with access to the room. To confirm his suspicions, Marty decided to review videotapes from a security camera in the hallway near the industrial arts room. On the tape, he saw Bob taking something out of the building to his car. It looked like something from the industrial arts room.

After showing the tape to the personnel director and the superintendent, Marty decided to confront Bob about the situation. He set a meeting date with Bob and carefully planned the conference. When the day arrived, Marty carefully laid out his conference and shared his suspicion about Bob. He told Bob that he would have to recommend that his employment be terminated. Of course, Bob was angry and denied stealing the equipment, but Marty did not back off. Finally, he showed Bob the videotape from the security camera. Bob admitted to "borrowing" the tools for a project. He asked if he could return the tools and if Marty could forget the incident. Marty told him he would accept Bob's resignation if he returned the equipment. Bob agreed, and the district decided not to press charges.

❖

In this scenario, Marty had to confront the issue of Bob potentially taking the equipment. He had to address Bob and personally deal with the behavior. This can be difficult to do but rewarding in the end because allowing the negative behavior to go on is unacceptable. As school leaders we must confront employee misconduct. In this chapter, you will learn about the following:

- the use of framing to constrain conversations when confronting behaviors
- selecting the proper words to use in naming and confronting employee issues
- how to use specific language tools to convey the seriousness of the issue
- taking advantage of your natural power when confronting behaviors
- developing precise and powerful written follow-up to verbal conferences

FRAMING

Framing is an effective tool to use when you have to meet and talk to an employee about poor performance or misconduct on the job. In framing, you as the speaker use words to draw a boundary around the conversation. See how the following statements work to set a boundary:

- "Today, we are here to talk about three issues I have with your performance."
- "In the past, I have addressed concerns about your attendance. Your behavior has not changed, so we need to talk about the next steps in the process of improvement."
- "I know that you and I have different perspectives on the severity of the issues we have discussed in the past, but since I'm your supervisor you need to follow my directives."

In each of these statements, the words spoken by the supervisor outline the boundaries of the conversation. We have found framing to be a highly effective tool for dealing with difficult employees because it helps to outline the parameters of the conversation, set a professional tone, and put you in charge as the supervisor. Figure 3.1 includes a blank framing planning template, and Figure 3.2 includes a completed sample to help illustrate this tool. Keep the following in mind as you deliver framing statements:

- Use framing as a strategy to start meetings or conferences.
- In designing your framing statement, consider the perspectives of the other person and the possible distractions this person may use to try to take you off topic.
- Plan an opening that sets parameters for the meeting or conference.
- As you deliver the statement, pause to allow the message to sink in and watch for the individual's reactions.
- Consider adding a hand gesture that matches and reinforces the intent of your framing statement.

Figure 3.1   Framing Statement Planning Template

Use this template to plan the framing statements you will use to keep your conversation on track when talking with a difficult employee.

When conferencing with difficult employees, one strategy they may try to employ is to take you off track. Framing statements draw parameters around the conversation and keep employees on track. As you complete this planning document, think about your previous interactions and experiences with the employee.

1. Employee name _____

2. How has this employee tried to take you off task or change a difficult conversation in past interactions?

   _____

   _____

3. In the spaces below, write down the distraction attempts you think you may encounter and the possible framing statements you may use to focus the conversation:

Possible Difficult Employee Distraction Attempts	Possible Framing Statements to Counter Distraction Attempt or Refocus Conversation After Attempt

| Figure 3.2 | Sample Completed Framing Statement Planning Template |

When conferencing with difficult employees, one strategy they may try to employ is to take you off track. Framing statements draw parameters around the conversation and keep employees on track. As you complete this planning document, think about your previous interactions and experiences with the employee.

1. Employee name: John Smith

2. How has this employee tried to take you off task or change a difficult conversation in past interactions? In past conversations, this employee has tried to bring up old issues or issues from the past that are not relevant.

3. In the spaces below, write down the distraction attempts you think you may encounter and the possible framing statements you may use to focus the conversation:

Possible Difficult Employee Distraction Attempts	Possible Framing Statements to Counter Distraction Attempt or Refocus Conversation After Attempt
"We never had to do this much work in the past."	"I know you and I have disagreed about the amount of work I have asked you to do, but workload cannot be an issue in this conversation. We have a reduced number of staff with higher expectations for performance."
"I've talked to people in other buildings, and they don't have to do this much at their schools."	"I know you have talked with colleagues at other schools and compared notes related to their workloads, but we have different conditions here."
"The previous principal said that I wouldn't get more work to do."	"I know you want me to honor promises made by Mrs. (name), but she is no longer here and the situation has changed since I have assumed leadership of this school."

Selecting the Proper Words to Use in Naming and Confronting Employee Issues

When addressing an employee's deficit behavior or misconduct, you need to select the right words to convey the seriousness of the situation. Let's see how Rory, a middle school principal, uses the proper words to define a situation she has with a teacher in the following example:

> As I review your progress throughout the year, I do know that you are trying, but your performance is still not meeting district standards in the area of making your lessons meaningful to your students.

Even though this is a simple and brief statement, Rory is clearly defining, through her use of the words she has chosen, that this teacher is not on track. "Not meeting district standards" is clear and direct. Let's look at the same scenario with less clarity used to define the performance:

As I review your performance throughout the year, I do know that you are trying, but I still have some concerns in the area of making your lessons meaningful to your students.

In reading this statement, you can see that the terms are a little less precise and there is room for interpretation. "Some concerns" may not communicate to the teacher the same level of deficit as "not meeting district standards" does.

When addressing deficit behavior or misconduct, keep the following in mind:

- Think through the severity of the situation you are trying to address.
- Identify the message you want the employee to get from your conversation.
- Select the proper words to convey the message and tone you want the employee to gain from your conversation.
- Write out a script or complete notes to help guide you as you meet with the employee and deliver the message.

The phrases listed in Figure 3.3 are some that we have used in our interactions with difficult employees in the past. Think through the unique situation you are facing, and select the phrases or wording that best fit your style and circumstances. Be sure your language matches the severity of the problem. Use the template in Figure 3.4 to help plan the language you will use to set the proper tone when delivering improvement messages to your employees.

Figure 3.5 shows a sample of a completed planning template.

Figure 3.3   Sample Wording to Convey Seriousness

As you think through your message to difficult or deficient employees, the words you select to describe the situation or behavior are crucial. Consider the following sample words to use when communicating your concern for their performance or behavior.

- does not meet district standards
- is deficient based on school expectations
- are not consistent with district performance expectations
- is getting in the way of your effectiveness as an employee
- are not in compliance with our expectations
- is not in compliance with what we agreed on in our earlier conference
- is not consistent with the performance of others
- are deficient based on our expectations
- needs your immediate attention
- if significant improvements can't be made I'll need to take further action
- since we have addressed this situation earlier you need to make immediate changes
- this is your last chance to improve before the situation escalates to the next level

Figure 3.4 Language Planning Template

Selecting the proper language when delivering improvement messages to employees is crucial to your success in communicating with them. As you complete this planning document, think about your previous interactions and experiences with the employee and assess this person's understanding of his or her improvement needs.

1. Employee name _____

2. Identify the severity of the deficiency related to the employee's job performance.

   _____

   _____

3. In the spaces below, list the severity of the performance deficits and the language you could use to properly label or identify it:

Employee Job Performance Deficits	Possible Framing Statements to Counter Distraction Attempt or Refocus Conversation After Attempt

| Figure 3.5 | Sample Completed Language Planning Template |

Selecting the proper language when delivering improvement messages to employees is crucial to your success in communicating with them. As you complete this planning document, think about your previous interactions and experiences with the employee and assess this person's understanding of his or her improvement needs.

1. Employee name: Joan Smith

2. Identify the severity of the deficiency related to the employee's job performance. Mrs. Smith is deficient in her work in assessing students and using the data to help her develop lessons. Mrs. Smith is also doing a poor job in communicating with parents and families. Several families have reported this, and I have had to deal with several situations in which parents were taken by surprise when their child's grade was reported at the end of the quarter. These issues may be related.

3. In the spaces below, list the severity of the performance deficits and the language you could use to properly label or identify it:

Employee Job Performance Deficits	Possible Framing Statements to Counter Distraction Attempt or Refocus Conversation After Attempt
Lack of understanding or use of assessment information in programming for instruction/lessons	"You don't appear to be using assessment data in your planning. This causes you to deliver poorly planned lessons. This situation is unacceptable and must be remedied immediately in the next week."
Lack of timely communication with parents	"You have not been communicating with parents in a timely manner. This performance is not meeting the standards of the district. You need to start (name strategies) immediately. Please send me a copy of your first communication next week."
Lack of timely communication with parents about their child's academic progress	"You have not been communicating with parents related to their children's performance in a timely manner. This performance is deficient and getting in the way of your effectiveness. You need to immediately start updating parents related to their child's performance.

AUTHORITY VOICE

When delivering difficult messages to employees, it is natural to be nervous and want to avoid confrontations. One thing we have found helpful over the years is to concentrate on the aspects of voice delivery that convey that we are the authority figure in the conversation. There are several aspects that you should pay attention to in relation to how you deliver a negative message:

- As you deliver your message, drop the pitch of your voice at the end of the statement. The dropping of the pitch will communicate to the receiver that you are the authority. When we hear a drop in pitch, we assume competence. TV newscasters use this skill effectively when delivering messages.

- Pace the speed you use in delivering your message. When you are in the position of communicating something negative with a person, it is natural to feel nervous and speed up your delivery. The increased speed can convey that nervousness or lack of confidence. Set a natural pace with your language to ensure clarity and a feeling of confidence.

- Pausing at key points can reinforce the seriousness of the issue. Consider building in purposeful pauses to provide an emphasis on key points in the delivery of a directive or negative message. Resist trying to fill in the pause time with unnecessary words or noises. Compare the difference in the following conversations:

"Today, I want to share some concerns I have with your performance. [Pause] The concerns revolve around three main issues. [Pause] The first issue is your attendance. [Pause] I have noticed that you have been late to work 15 times in the past three months. That rate is unacceptable. [Pause] We have talked about this issue before, and you have shared your excuses for not being at work on time. Today I am not interested in talking about why you are late. I will share the consequences I have determined for that behavior. [Pause]"

In this conversation, the pauses were inserted by the person delivering the message to reinforce the main points she wanted to make. The silence experienced as a result of the pauses allowed a few seconds for the receiver of the message to think about the consequences of the behavior.

Let's look at the same conversation, but omitting the pauses and filling in the gap with words and noises. See if you notice a difference in the message being communicated.

"Today, I want to share some concerns I have with your performance. OK? [Clears throat] The concerns revolve around three main issues, you know? The first issue is about your attendance. What are your thoughts about your attendance? [Employee says he has been trying really hard to get to work on time.] I have noticed that you have been late to work 15 times in the past three months. That rate is unacceptable. Don't you think so? [Employee shares that nothing happens at the beginning of the day anyway.] We have talked about this issue before, and you have shared your excuses for not being at work on time. Today I am not interested in talking about why you are late. I will share the consequences I have determined for that behavior. OK?"

In the second example, you can see that the supervisor is a little less sure of herself as a result of the language she is using. When she fills in the gap in language with "OK?' and asks "What are your thoughts?" she provides an opening for the employee and diminishes her authority as a supervisor.

Taking Advantage of Your Natural Power When Confronting Behaviors

With your position as a principal come natural power elements that you can use in dealing with deficient or difficult employees. Your state and the fact that you are licensed to practice your craft reinforce your authority as a supervisor. Take advantage of this natural power associated with your position. Here are some ideas for increasing your use of the power afforded by your position:

- Reference your role as the supervisor when you deliver negative messages or directives. Stating "As your supervisor . . ." or "In my role as the principal . . ." can help reinforce your positional power.
- Deliver directives while sitting behind your desk. Your desk and its position have a natural power connotation. You can take advantage of this when delivering a negative message. If you want to set a collaborative tone, sit side by side with the other person. This position conveys a partnership.
- Consider dressing formally when delivering a negative message. Wearing a suit or other professional dress reinforces the power of your position.

Developing Precise and Powerful Written Follow-Up to Conferences

Verbal directives and messages have power, but following up with clear written communication reinforces the verbal message you delivered. When constructing written communication, keep the following points in mind:

- Make sure your written communication is an accurate account of the verbal conference. Choose wording and phrasing carefully to make sure it is an exact summary of the events and conversation from the conference. If your account is inaccurate or if you add things that you forgot to say, your credibility can be undermined.
- While maintaining accuracy, be clear and direct in your use of words in your summary. When your wording wanders off topic or you use

too many words to share your message, your written summary becomes distracting. This level of distraction takes away from your power as the principal and supervisor.

- Use bullet points and summary statements to reinforce main ideas and directives.
- Be sure your timelines and other points are presented in a sequential manner. Make sure the written document is easy to follow and makes sense to the reader.

Employees need to know that you are giving them a direct order when you give a directive. Keep the following points in mind as you deliver a directive to an employee:

- Be clear and concise in your choice of words.
- Use statements such as "I am directing you . . ." or "I need to . . ." or "You have to . . ."
- Check to make sure that the employee understands the directive and knows what to do.
- Make sure that what you have directed the employee to do is reasonable and possible.
- Set up a deadline for the directive to be completed.
- Follow up in writing to document your directive.

Effective directives clearly communicate your expectations to your employees. Figure 3.6 provides a direct planning template. Review the following statements to decide whether they meet the criteria for effective directives.

- Please do the following by 10 a.m. Wednesday . . .
- Would you mind responding by . . .
- I insist that you . . .
- You are directed to . . .
- I would appreciate it if you would . . .
- Perhaps you should . . .
- I expect the following by . . .
- You are hereby required to . . .
- You may wish to . . .
- The report is due by . . .
- It would be helpful if you would . . .
- I insist that you consider the following . . .

If communicated correctly, directives have the power to clearly let employees know what is expected and the timeline for the expectation to be fulfilled. If expectations are not communicated clearly, you leave room for interpretation. A large part of your power as a supervisor is related to the perception of your effectiveness. By constructing and communicating clear directives, you increase your power as a supervisor.

Figure 3.6   Directive Planning Template

Use this template to plan clear and purposeful directives. Be sure to assess your written directives to make sure they met the criteria for effectiveness.

When giving a directive, make sure your statements are clear and that they are truly directives. As you think about the employee and the situation, complete the following prompts to assist you in your design.

1. Employee name _____

2. What specifically do you need the employee to do or stop doing as a result of your directive?

   _____

3. Write a draft of your directive here:

   _____

   _____

   _____

4. Review your directive, assessing it for the following:

   _____ Clarity

   _____ Specificity

   _____ Understandable by employee

   _____ Truly a directive

   _____ Uses the fewest words possible to convey the message

5. Use this space to refine the directive:

   _____

   _____

   _____

Nice check list

SUMMARY

In this chapter, we have presented tools to assist you as you approach difficult situations and address employee deficiencies and misconduct. As you think about these strategies and skills, respond to the following questions:

- How can I use my natural power as the supervisor to help make difficult conversations easier to deliver?
- What aspects about my voice delivery do I need to keep in mind as I plan to deliver negative messages?
- What ideas do I need to consider when writing follow-up documents in order to reinforce difficult conversations and conferences?

As you consider delivering a difficult conference, keep in mind the information you have learned in this chapter. In Chapter 4, you will learn self-protection strategies that will help you feel safe and stay on track as you work with difficult and deficient staff members to improve their behavior or to move toward termination.

NOTES

Write any notes that you think might be helpful to you as you implement the strategies/ideas presented in this chapter with your difficult employees. Feel free to refer back to these notes as you need to when confronting their issues or behaviors.

_____

_____

_____

_____

_____

_____

_____

_____

_____

_____

_____

_____

_____

_____

4

Protecting Yourself While Dealing With Difficult Employees

S elf-protection is essential when you are considering confronting a deficient or difficult employee. In this chapter we present ideas and strategies that will help you as you confront difficult employees and situations. As you read this chapter you will learn about the following:

- tools that can offer you some degree of protection from the negative energy exhibited by difficult, angry people
- methods to displace or divert negative energy away from you so you can concentrate on delivering your message
- using the natural power afforded to you by your position to assist you in delivering a negative message

PRESUPPOSITIONS

Presuppositions, when used properly, can help you when conferencing with marginal employees by shifting responsibility from you to the employee. Presuppositions are language tools that help communicate to the subconscious part of the employee's brain and can be used to shape thinking or behavior in others. These tools include strategically placed words, pauses, and emphasis or intonation used when delivering directives or answering questions. Consider this example:

- "**You** are the one person who can fix this situation." In this example the word *you* is emphasized, strongly communicating that the person you are addressing has the power to solve the problem.

Here is another example with a slightly different meaning to be interpreted from the different intonation or emphasis:

- "You are the **one** person who can fix this situation." In this example, the word *one* is emphasized, strongly communicating that the person you are addressing is the only person with the power to solve the problem. Singling out a person as the one who can solve the problem can be very motivating.

Finally, this third example shows yet another interpretation based on where the emphasis is placed in the sentence:

- "You are the one person who can **fix** this situation." In this example, the word *fix* is emphasized, communicating that the person being spoken to has the ability to solve or fix the problem, whereas others who try may just be able to temporarily address the issue.

Emphasis or intonation is one way that you as a supervisor can make the seriousness of a particular situation known. Using intonation also helps protect you because you project the problem into the employee's court rather than take on the responsibility for that person's problem or deficiency. Try inserting emphasis when you want to clearly communicate the seriousness of the issue. Here are some specific examples illustrating this point:

- What will you do to improve your performance?
- My role is to inform you of the issue; your role is to work on getting better.
- What will you do to significantly improve your performance?

In addition to emphasis, another way that presuppositions work is by using specific words or word order to communicate an employee's role in dealing with issues. In using this type of presupposition, you plant a seed in the employee's head based on selecting words to empower her subconscious to take action. Consider how the following statements help to clearly outline the employee's role or responsibility in solving the problem through the use of selected words:

- "As you think about how you'll do . . ." (The key here is *think*. When you say the word, the employee subconsciously gets the message that you believe she can think about the next steps.)
- "What are your plans for . . ." (By purposely using the word *plans,* you are communicating that you believe the employee can plan.)
- "What will you need as you begin to solve . . ." (By adding *begin* and *solve,* you informally communicate that you believe the employee can start to solve the issue.)
- "Share your next steps for . . ." (You are saying that you believe the employee can develop the necessary steps to deal with the issue at hand.)
- "In relation to this situation, what will be your first step . . ." (By asking for the first step, you are helping the employee break the issue down into steps and asking for the first one in the series.)
- "What is your role in . . ." (You are communicating that the problem is owned by the employee.) — office issue ?
- "What will you do to address . . ." (You are communicating that the employee needs to develop something to address the issue.)
- "This is what is expected. How will you meet the expectations for . . ." (You are communicating the expectations and then getting commitment from the employee to meet those expectations.)

Over the years, in both our own work and our work with others, we have found presuppositions to be extremely valuable in shaping conversations. They have also helped as we have tried to move responsibility for performance issues from us to the employee. A statement like "As you think about the main points of our conference today, what key elements will you use to move forward?" lets an employee know that you expect him to focus on the key points while also moving forward to improve his performance. See Figure 4.1 for a template on using suppositions.

REFLECTING

We find that reflecting back the emotions/content of an angry or upset person's message goes a long way in lowering the level of anger. This is a self-protection skill to help you, because if her anger is reflected back it will not negatively impact you. We also use this skill when we have to deliver negative messages in order to help us convey that we understand what the person we are talking to has said and feels. Allowing a person to feel heard is another important aspect of self-protection for you as the supervisor. At times, angry or upset people lower their negative energy when they feel they have at least been heard. There are three basic forms of reflecting that we use in our work with difficult or angry people.

Figure 4.1	Planning Template for Using Presuppositions in Employee Conferences

Presuppositions can be valuable tools in communicating with difficult employees. Use this template to plan your use of presuppositions in your employee conferences.

1. List the issues you are planning to confront in this conference.

_____

_____

_____

2. What is the employee's responsibility in owning these issues or his or her positive resolution?

_____

_____

_____

3. What words or phrases might resonate with this person to help him or her focus on the issue at hand? What words will you want to emphasize in order to clearly communicate your expectations when working with this person?

_____

_____

_____

Content Reflecting

With this type of reflecting, you are in essence returning the content the sender told you but are reflecting it back after translating it. The statement you make to reflect it should be synonymous with the original statement but not just repeat the exact words of the speaker. Review the examples in Figure 4.2.

| Figure 4.2 | Content Reflecting Examples |

The sender said . . .	A content reflecting statement might be . . .
"I have a concern about the number of students assigned to my classroom, the makeup of the students, and a lack of materials I have to use in my teaching."	"You shared your three main concerns about your assignment that included student numbers, how the boys and girls are distributed, and the fact that you don't have what you need in order to teach effectively."
"I am upset with your assessment of my performance on the job and how you don't seem positive and supportive of me."	"Your major concerns are related to my formal feedback and the fact that you don't feel I am positive about your efforts."
"My previous principal allowed me to work in whatever manner I wanted as long as I got my job completed."	"You shared your preference for how you were evaluated in the past compared to how I am doing it."
"You don't know how difficult it is to concentrate on all of my tasks in addition to having to take care of my other team members."	"You are busy doing several other tasks in addition to taking care of your own classroom."

The examples listed in Figure 4.2 are for illustration only, and they use our words. If you are considering content reflecting as a strategy, be sure to use words that are comfortable for you. The core idea we are trying to illustrate here is that you can help the employee feel heard, lower her anger level, and help her relax and be better prepared to hear your message as a result of using content reflecting. Also, content reflecting is useful because once an employee has heard what he just said, it can de-escalate the negative emotions associated with the improvement message. This is an important skill that you can use to help protect you from the negative energy associated with receiving an improvement message.

Emotional Reflecting

This is another type of reflecting that we have found to be helpful in our work with difficult employees. In emotional reflecting, you as the receiver listen to the employee and hear comments that give you a clue about her emotional state. Instead of just reflecting what you heard, you reflect the emotion behind the comment. By doing so, you help the employee feel heard and help de-escalate her anger. This can help protect you from attack because you communicate to the employee that you understand how she is feeling. Look at the examples in Figure 4.3, and see how the emotion is clearly labeled. We used the same sender statements as in Figure 4.2 to illustrate how to implement emotional reflecting with almost any statement.

Figure 4.3	Emotional Reflecting Examples

The sender said . . .	An emotional reflecting statement might be . . .
"I have a concern about the number of students assigned to my classroom, the makeup of the students, and a lack of materials I have to use in my teaching."	"You are frustrated with your current situation."
"I am upset with your assessment of my performance on the job and how you don't seem positive and supportive of me."	"You are upset with my evaluation report."
"My previous principal allowed me to work in whatever manner I wanted as long as I got my job completed."	"You feel as though you aren't being treated as fairly as you were in the past."
"You don't know how difficult it is to concentrate on all of my tasks in addition to having to take care of my other team members."	"You are overwhelmed with all of the work you have had to do here."

Integrating Reflecting

At times, difficult employees will tell you a flurry of complaints or grievances. These people can get lost in the number of complaints and can benefit from someone helping them see the general themes or trends in their complaints. The concept of integrating reflecting combines the seemingly unrelated complaints into a package in order to assist the employee in seeing how they are related and fit together. Look at the examples in Figure 4.4.

Figure 4.4	Integrating Reflecting Examples

The sender said . . .	An integrating reflecting statement might be . . .
"I have a concern about the number of students assigned to my classroom, the makeup of the students, and a lack of materials I have to use in my teaching."	"The three points you made were all related to your ability to positively impact your students."
"I am upset with your assessment of my performance on the job and how you don't seem positive and supportive of me."	"In general, you have shared ideas related to your performance as a teacher."
"My previous principal allowed me to work in whatever manner I wanted as long as I got my job completed."	"You shared several concerns in this meeting, but they all related to how I treat you versus how your previous supervisor treated you."
"You don't know how difficult it is to concentrate on all of my tasks in addition to having to take care of my other team members."	"First you shared the tasks that you need to do in order to help your team members, and then you shared how this focus took you away from your own preparation time."

We have found reflecting to be an important tool in helping us and the leaders we have supported work successfully with difficult employees. Use the various types of reflecting as a form of self-protection and to redirect employee comments and anger.

DISPLACING NEGATIVE ENERGY

When we have to deliver negative messages, we find that if we are looking at the person while we are talking, her negative energy is directly transmitted to us. At times, this transmission of negative energy can penetrate our mind and distract us from the focus we are trying to set up in the meeting. One method we use to avoid this distraction is to displace the negative energy, that is, we try to move the focus off of us and onto another object. Normally we write the concerns on a piece of paper and then hold the paper off to the side between us and the person who is getting the negative message so that we can both look at it together (see Figure 4.5). As we both look at the list of concerns, we verbally outline them. She is focused on looking at the paper and not at us, so her negative energy is focused on the paper. This method makes it much more comfortable to deliver a negative message than looking the other person in the eye.

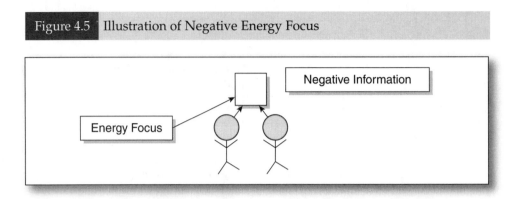

Figure 4.5   Illustration of Negative Energy Focus

ADDITIONAL SELF-PROTECTION STRATEGIES

When you are confronting negative people, they could try to attack you both personally and emotionally. If difficult people think that they can attack you and take you off track, you will not be able to keep the pressure on them. Their goal is to undermine your confidence so you cannot deal with the real issues at hand. As hard as it is to do, you need to find ways to protect yourself emotionally when you are under attack from these difficult people. Consider the following strategies.

Remember Your Role and Position in the Organizational Hierarchy

As the principal of the school, you are in a supervisory position. Keep this in mind as you work with difficult staff members. You have the right to confront them about performance issues and to talk with them about your intention for them to improve their work performance. Many times, we tend to forget this as supervisors and we let employees have the upper hand. In the supervisor/supervisee relationship, the person being supervised needs to treat you with respect and dignity. If these two things don't happen, we have the right to confront the person, address the negative behavior, and close down the meeting. Before meeting with a potentially difficult person, keep in mind who is the supervisor and who is the employee in the situation.

Block Negative Energy From Entering Your Mind

Our minds are powerful in selecting what we do and don't pay attention to in our conversations with others. As you meet with difficult people, think about the potential negative statements that they will make to you and about you, and prepare yourself to block these from entering your mind. Some people engage in self-talk strategies to help them block negative statements. Internal self-talk statements such as "That's not true" or "I am not accepting that" can go a long way toward keeping potentially harmful statements from entering your mind as you work with negative people. In the past, we have even gone as far as internally "tuning out" another person and their comments in order to keep them from entering our minds.

Reflect Emotions/Content Back to the Person Attacking You

Even though this strategy was discussed earlier in this chapter, it is repeated here to illustrate the differences and advantages related to paraphrasing. This strategy involves using a skill closely related to paraphrasing, but it is different due to the directness of the reflecting statement. Here are some examples:

Reflecting Statements

- "You are really angry."
- "The main point you are trying to make is . . ."
- "You are upset about this."
- "Your main objections are . . ."
- "Your major concern is . . ."
- "This is unnerving for you."
- "Your three biggest objections are . . ."

As you can see from these examples, the statements are very direct in how they are worded. We have found that being direct works well when dealing with difficult people. The following are the same statements, but they have been softened and turned into paraphrasing statements. As you read through them, examine how they are different than the reflecting statements.

Paraphrasing Statements

- "I feel that you're really angry."
- "My perception is that the main point you're trying to make is . . ."
- "I am picking up that you are upset about this."
- "I perceive that your main objections are . . ."
- "I feel that your major concern is . . ." ✓
- "It seems to me that this is unnerving for you."
- "I have picked up that your three biggest objections are . . ."

These paraphrasing examples address the same kinds of concerns that were addressed by reflecting statements but in a less direct manner. As we mentioned earlier, in our experience reflecting statements work better then paraphrasing statements. We have found that many of the extremely difficult people we've worked with have heard paraphrasing statements for a number of years. When we've tried using paraphrasing statements with them, some would be immediately turned off and roll their eyes. The reflecting statements seem to better match the higher emotions sometimes exhibited by difficult people and protect you as the person delivering the negative message from the emotions of the person receiving the message. However, you need to use the strategies that you are most comfortable with and that match the situation you're in at a given time.

Set and Follow Clear Parameters in a Meeting With a Difficult Person

As you think about meeting with a difficult or extremely negative employee, it's important that you take the time to set clear parameters to make the meeting a safe place for both you and the employee. Clear parameters protect you from emotional attack as you deliver improvement messages to an employee. By staying clear and direct, you will be better able to deliver your intended message in a manner that is understandable to the employee. One way to establish clear parameters is to incorporate the use of ground rules. The beginning of the meeting is a good time to lay out a few simple and easy-to-follow ground rules. Here are some examples of ground rules we have used in past meetings:

- Everyone will be allowed to share his or her perspective without being interrupted during this meeting.
- During the meeting, voice levels will be kept at a conversational level.
- The agenda for the meeting will be followed in order.
- Each person will get a chance to ask questions and respond to questions in the meeting.
- The meeting will focus only on professional behaviors; the meeting will not be used to discuss or solve personal issues.
- At the end of the meeting, a written summary of the major agreements and accomplishments will be written.
- If a question or issue comes up in the meeting that one or both parties cannot address, they will be given a chance to gather information about this issue and bring it back to a future meeting.

Ground rules are good because they help keep the meeting on track and focused on the issues that need to be addressed. When you are in charge of a conference with a difficult employee, it is a good idea to have several of your potential ground rules written out so that you can discuss them with the employee and show him a copy. This process helps everyone in a meeting remember the ground rules and stay on track.

Use Gesturing to Move Negative Energy Away From You

Nonverbal communication in the form of gestures is extremely powerful in helping to protect you from taking on the negative energy generated by difficult people. In a powerful way, gestures let others know of your intention to take on their issues. Each gesture communicates to the subconscious brain of the person seeing it. In many cases, we are able to diffuse most of the negative energy in a person just by using a gesture. Here are some of the more common gestures that we use when we want to move negative energy away from us:

Hand held out in front of you, palm facing the difficult person. This gesture is associated with telling people to stop. When we use this gesture, we normally hold the hand between chest and eye level. It is very effective in blocking negative energy.

Hand starting at midpoint of body, palm facing your chest, sweeping outward toward the difficult person. This gesture acts as a sweeping motion to push away negative energy. At the end of the gesture, your hand is actually pointing toward the person with your palm facing outward, which can communicate openness.

Index finger pointing. At times, we have found it difficult to break in to a conversation with a difficult person who is extremely angry. We point our index finger at our chest when we feel it is our turn to speak. In many cases, this gesture has actually stopped the person from speaking so that we can get our point across. At times, we may have to say, "It is my turn to speak," in conjunction with this gesture.

Figure 4.6 summarizes some of the more common gestures and meanings.

Figure 4.6   Common Gestures and Their Meanings

- Hand held in front of facilitator, palm toward audience = Stop.
- Arm and hand extended toward group or individual = Refers to group or individual.
- Hand and arm move toward speaker, palm toward speaker = Refers to me.
- Arm and hand rotate horizontally in a circle = All of us together.
- Finger pointed = Refers to person or object pointed at.
- Arm and hand sweep away from body toward chart or other visual = Please refer to this.
- Hands and arms out away from the body = Welcome and open to ideas.
- Fingers held in numerical arrangement = Order or position in sequence.
- Hand out in front, palms held up = Open for suggestions or unsure about information.

Source: Eller, 2004.

Use Your Position to Gain Power

Many times, we forget that our body position is an excellent tool to use when dealing with difficult people. Depending on how you position yourself, you can control the energy and keep negative energy from getting to you and throwing your conference off track. Here are some of the more common body positions we have found to be effective when dealing with difficult people:

Standing in a doorway. Some extremely difficult people try to position themselves so that they are standing in a doorway, backing you into a wall or a closed room. In dealing with this type of person, it is extremely effective to have her enter a room or office and then you stand in the doorway to deliver your reprimand or message. In this position, your body is between her and the exit to the room. This is helpful because you are now in control of the situation, and the difficult person cannot just spout off and then leave through the exit.

Standing while the difficult person is sitting. This can be another extremely effective position to use when dealing with a difficult person. When you are standing, you have natural power over someone who is sitting. This natural power may help you control the conference and avoid being attacked emotionally by the difficult employee. Sometimes, a difficult person will figure this out and stand up partly through the conference. You may want to start off by standing next to him and then gradually moving to sit down. This helps establish power at the beginning of the meeting but also lets him know that you're willing to work with him on a more collaborative basis after the initial issues are out on the table.

Meeting in a room with a small table, having the difficult person sit with her back to the wall. This scenario is somewhat like standing in the doorway. Your body is between the difficult person and the exit again, so you control the meeting. You can stay on message and focused because the natural power you gain as a result of your body positioning is effective in communicating who is in charge during this conference. By taking advantage of your natural power, you can work from an offensive base rather than having to react to the changing landscape.

Sitting behind your desk, using your positional power. This position is a classic; many principals have used this over the years to help gain power over difficult people. The larger and more intimidating your desk is, the better this technique works.

Sitting at a table with your chair set higher than the employee's chair. This strategy is related to standing while the other person is sitting. The difference in height based on the two chairs causes some level of power and ultimately intimidation of the other party.

Stop the Meeting; Tell the Person That You Will Not Move on Until He Calms Down

This strategy is quite obvious. As a leader or supervisor, simply state that the meeting cannot continue until the person decides to calm down and rationally discuss the issue. Sometimes, you may have to repeat this several times or even begin to walk away from the meeting before he gets the message that you will not continue with his present emotional state in place.

Use Framing Statements to Set Parameters for the Interaction

Framing statements can be highly effective in dealing with difficult people and channeling negative energy away from you as a supervisor. In putting together framing statements, is important that you construct them so that they clearly communicate the parameters of the discussion. Look over the following statements, and think about how they clearly communicate the parameters of a meeting:

- "In our discussion today, we will only be looking at positive solutions we can implement in the future. We will not be spending time revisiting the problems of the past."
- "I know you want to spend time talking about your relationship problems with your supervisor, but in this meeting we will only be focusing on how to fairly divide the workload."
- "I know that there are many things we need to talk about, but in today's meeting we will only be focusing on how you can work more effectively with the groups renting our gym."
- "There are many problems that we need to solve. We're only going to focus on those related to your work assignment. If we are successful in putting together a plan to solve those items and we have time left in our meeting, we will begin to look at the other issues that you have mentioned."

Pace Your Voice Speed

The speed of your voice can do a lot to both protect you and de-escalate extremely negative or emotional situations. As you start a conversation with a difficult person, make sure that your voice speed is somewhat similar to hers. By pacing with her, you send her a subconscious message that you understand and that you're communicating with her. After you've connected effectively, you can begin to gradually slow down your voice to help lead her to a calmer state. We have found this strategy to be particularly helpful in calming down people who were previously out of control.

Control Your Internal Emotional State

One of the best defenses that you can have against extremely emotional or difficult people is control over your own internal emotional state. This is helpful because you are able to listen to what they have to say without letting it get to you. Controlling your own internal emotional state takes some practice but in the end can help you avoid getting caught up in the emotions of the immediate conversation. We have found that when we are practicing controlling our own internal emotional state, the concentration needed for that task helps us stay focused and better able to hold off the negative emotions that the difficult person is trying to put on us.

SUMMARY

Self-protection is one of the most crucial skills you can use and practice when dealing with difficult employees. As you may remember from our earlier discussions, one of the ways difficult employees avoid dealing with their deficiencies is to take you off track. If you aren't able to stay focused while delivering the improvement or termination message, the employee will be let off the hook. Mastering self-protection strategies is also important because it can help lower your nervousness and increase the chance that you will successfully confront negative employee performance or behavior issues. Think about your responses to the following questions as you reflect on your learning from this chapter:

- What are the various kinds of reflecting, and how can they help you as you work with difficult employees?
- What is framing, and how can this strategy help keep a difficult meeting or conversation focused and professional?
- What other kinds of professional power tools discussed in this chapter can you use to keep difficult conversations on track and professional?

The strategies presented so far in this book are designed to work with employees from any of the major groups present in schools. These skills are generic in nature and will even work with groups outside of the school. In the second half of this book, we will focus on the major employee groups that you encounter in a school setting. Each chapter will focus specifically on some of the unique characteristics and challenges that these employee groups may pose to you as the school leader. We will present a new group in each individual chapter along with the direct applications and variations needed specifically for it.

NOTES

Write any notes that you think might be helpful to you as you implement the strategies/ideas presented in this chapter with your difficult employees. Feel free to refer back to these notes as you need to when confronting their issues or behaviors.

_____

_____

_____

_____

_____

_____

_____

_____

_____

_____

_____

_____

_____

_____

5

Strategies for Working With Difficult/ Marginal Teachers

❖

Dennis, a high school principal, has a physical education teacher on his staff that is not following the school's expectations related to the supervision of students. He has heard from other staff members, parents, and teachers that this teacher is very negative with children and is constantly yelling at them. He also understands that she sometimes leaves the classroom to stop by the teachers' lounge, leaving her class unattended. He decides that he needs to address these behaviors for the good of the students and the school.

Dennis sets up a meeting with the teacher, Beverly, and clearly addresses his concerns. He has developed a conference plan to let Beverly know what his concerns are and his expectations for her improvement. He frames his ideas as directives with clear and attainable timelines.

After six months of work, Beverly still sneaks around and leaves her class unattended. She also gets angry and yells at students. After taking her through the first steps of the employee discipline protocol, Dennis decides it is time to provide more formal notification and assistance.

Dennis issues Beverly a letter of deficiency clearly outlining her deficient behaviors and timelines for her to improve. When he calls her to the office to deliver the letter to her, she refuses to enter and states that she does not want to take the letter from Dennis. He asks his administrative assistant to be a witness to the interaction and see that Beverly will not take the deficiency letter even though he has offered it to her. He directs Beverly to stay in the office area and verbally tells her that he is delivering a letter of deficiency to her and the contents of the letter. As he tries to hand the letter to her (at the doorway of the office), Beverly lets the letter drop to the floor. Rather than getting in a fight, Dennis decides to just turn away and walk back to his office. As he walks away, Beverly slowly bends over and picks up the letter. She quietly leaves the office.

Dennis continues to check on her class and her progress in eliminating negative yelling and staying to supervise students. Beverly now knows that Dennis means business, but she also feels that she cannot make the kind of changes he is requiring. After consultation with her union representative, she decides to take advantage of an early retirement incentive being offered by the school district. She completes the paperwork and submits it to the district office but does not tell Dennis. He is informed by the district office of her application. He continues to work with Beverly, and at the end of the year she leaves the building. She does not talk to Dennis and leaves the school angry and upset. He is able to hire a new teacher to take her place who is more focused on students and supervision.

A large portion of the employee interaction we have as principals and supervisors is with teachers. While entire books have been written about working with difficult or negative teachers, this chapter is designed to provide concise and direct information related to this employee group. The material in this chapter will focus on the following aspects of working with difficult teachers:

- the importance of understanding evaluation criteria
- why you need to be able to clearly describe the reasons why you feel that a teacher's performance is deficient
- focusing on base and surface competencies in working with teachers
- deciding whether to develop a growth plan or move to possible termination
- delivering a conference to discuss performance issues or possible termination

Working with deficient teachers can be extremely challenging. In your role as a supervisor, you need to be able to confront people when they are not performing their job in a manner that meets the standards established in the building or district. Teachers can be a difficult group to work with because of their professional nature and the blanket of protection that most states provide for teachers. Let's briefly look at some of these issues.

THE LAW AND TEACHER EMPLOYMENT

Let us start off with some good general advice for dealing with teacher performance issues. Spend some time getting to know and understand the teacher employment laws for your particular state. This can be done by talking with someone in your personnel department, your superintendent, an attorney, a school law professor, or someone in your state administrators' association. You need to develop a thorough and comprehensive understanding of how the employment and termination laws in your state work so that you clearly know what to do as you move forward. The following concepts and terms are provided as a general guide for you to consider as you begin to work with difficult, marginal, or deficient teachers. Be sure you do enough research to feel comfortable working with the laws, policies, and rules pertaining to teacher employment so that you can move forward with confidence and competence when you encounter a deficient or marginal teacher.

Employment Status

We have had the opportunity to work as administrators in several states during our careers and to study the statutes related to teacher employment in several others. In most states, there are clear distinctions related to employment. As we said earlier, be sure to read and understand your state's laws and rules before moving forward with any action. In working with teachers, you need to understand two of the most common employment status distinctions: probationary and continuing contract.

Probationary. In several states a teacher is considered a probationary employee when he is first hired by a school district. The length of time can vary, but several states outline a three-year probationary period for new teachers. A probationary period is a process that is designed to let the district try out an employee to see whether he will be a good fit. During the probationary period, the district has more discretion or freedom to terminate employment if the employee is not meeting the needs or expectations laid out for him. If a termination occurs, the employee is still guaranteed due process rights. Some people may refer to this type of employee as *non-tenured*, though most states do not use that terminology.

Continuing contract. Once an employee has successfully completed the probationary period and been declared as meeting the expectations of the district, she is normally granted continuing contract status. This means that she has been evaluated and is meeting expectations. This employee has a reasonable expectation or right to continue her employment in the district. Some people refer to this type of employee as being tenured or having tenure.

Obviously, the contract status of the teacher has a lot to do with your approach and ultimate success in working with this person. If you are dealing with someone who is in a probationary situation, it is much easier to terminate his employment than it is if he has attained continuing contract status. As we work with principals who are terminating continuing contract teachers, they constantly tell us, "I feel like I'm on trial rather than the deficient teacher!" This is because once a teacher has been granted continuing contract status, he has in essence been found to be competent in relation to district expectations. As far as the state goes, this teacher is competent. If you determine that this same teacher is not competent, you will have to prove that this is the case. So you should feel like you are on trial since you are refuting the teacher's previously competent rating or determination.

Understanding the implications of probationary and continuing contract status is crucial when working with teachers. When working with a probationary teacher, it is important to spend the time necessary to really get to know whether the teacher is competent and meeting district teaching standards. If you have any doubts in relation to an employee's actual or potential performance, you need to take action before he reaches continuing contract status. Contrary to popular belief, it is not impossible to terminate a teacher who has reached continuing contract status; it just takes more thought, planning, and time to accomplish this task. We will provide more information related to this aspect later in the chapter.

Conditions for Possible Contract Nonrenewal

In most states, there are clearly articulated reasons or conditions that can be used to terminate the employment of a teacher. As we mentioned earlier, be sure to check the specific statutes in your state, talk with someone in your personnel department, or visit with an attorney for more information before you move forward on teacher termination. In general, most states allow continuing contract teachers to be terminated for the following reasons:

- *Insubordination:* If you give an employee a directive or direct order and she chooses to ignore you, the stage could be set for insubordination. The definition for insubordination varies by state, but in general it can be grounds for dismissal. Be sure to check your state statutes or check with your personnel department or an attorney before looking at this option for the termination. Over the years, as we have helped principals with this aspect of teacher termination, we have had to take the following into consideration:
  - Did the principal give an order or directive?
  - Was the order or directive reasonable, and was it within the teacher's ability to follow it?
  - Was the directive given to address a serious situation or condition?

If the insubordinate act is serious enough, you could have grounds for termination of the teacher's contract. Specific strategies for giving clear directives are outlined on page 36 of Chapter 3.

• *Immorality:* Teachers are in a position that gives them contact with and influence over children, so they need to act in the highest regard when it comes to their moral behavior. Teachers have been terminated for issues related to their moral behavior, such as viewing inappropriate Web sites, viewing pornographic material, making inappropriate advances and having inappropriate relationships with students, and making inappropriate comments in the classroom. Even though the media would have us think otherwise, thankfully, in light of the numbers of teachers there are in the United States, these incidents are rare. If you suspect a situation or it is reported to you that a teacher has engaged or is engaging in immoral behavior, you need to investigate and take immediate action. Check with your district personnel department, your superintendent, or an attorney right away for specific guidance on how to proceed. We will provide a general guide for dealing with this type of situation later in this chapter, but you should seek out local information from a competent source so you can design a plan that meets your needs.

• *Incompetence/inefficiency:* If a teacher is not doing an effective job of teaching students, he may be able to be terminated using the incompetence/ inefficiency provision of employment statutes. This is probably the most commonly used reason for teacher terminations, but it takes extensive documentation and work to put together a case for termination due to incompetence. As we talked about earlier in this chapter, when it comes to continuing contract teachers, you have to prove that they are incompetent or inefficient at the present time when someone previously certified that they are competent based on evaluation and their successful completion of the probationary period. Dealing with this type of situation is the major focus of this chapter.

YOUR MASTER CONTRACT OR MASTER AGREEMENT

Most school districts, whether they are located in unionized states or right-to-work (or nonunionized) states, operate with some kind of master agreement. Since the teaching staff is normally the largest employee group in the district, the district and the board operate from a common set of expectations and rules. Before you take on a marginal or deficient teacher, you need to review this master agreement. It will normally specify the conditions for teacher evaluation, the various components in the teacher evaluation system, the timelines for processes such as observation visits, the number of evaluations that should be conducted, the timelines and procedures for notifications, the procedures for teacher rebuttals, and so on.

It's obviously a good idea to thoroughly read and understand all of the components of the master agreement in relation to teacher evaluation. It's also crucial to be sure that you are implementing the components fairly and consistently with your teaching staff. We have seen principals get themselves into trouble by trying to focus on a deficient teacher without consistently following the guidelines used with others in the past. Consider this example:

Mike, a high school principal, suspected that one of his math teachers was not doing a good job in implementing the curriculum. He decided to spend time observing the teacher and soon found that his suspicions were true. When he decided to met with the teacher to talk about the situation in the classroom, the teacher asked for a union member to sit in on the conference as a representative. As Mike started to talk about the deficiencies he found in the math teacher's classroom, the union representative asked Mike to provide the date of the fall evaluation orientation session he had held to explain the expectations and processes that would be used in this year's teacher evaluation process. Mike had to say that he hadn't provided the orientation. The union representative told Mike that by not conducting an orientation meeting, he was in violation of the master agreement. If Mike pressed the issue of the math class, the union would be forced to file a grievance. Mike had to back away from his effort to work with this teacher because he had forgotten to follow the master contract requirement about providing an orientation meeting.

It may sound like the teacher got off the hook too easily, but if you don't follow the conditions set forth in your master agreement, you could be opening yourself up to a potential problem down the road when you need to move forward on working with a deficient teacher. The moral of the story is to read, understand, and fully implement all aspects related to your master agreement.

UNDERSTANDING YOUR EVALUATION CRITERIA

One of the key concepts we have found that helps determine your success as a leader in confronting negative behavior is your knowledge of teacher evaluation criteria. In most school systems today, clear criteria are used to evaluate teachers. There are also administrative procedures governing work attendance, completion of lesson plans, and so on. For your survival as a leader, you need to clearly understand these standards and be able to articulate them to others. Here are some strategies that leaders have used to gain a more comprehensive understanding of the standards by which teachers are evaluated:

- Read through the evaluation and performance criteria; write down examples to illustrate or share what they would look like in operation.

- Each week, take a small number of the evaluation and performance standards and place them on a note card. As you do walk-through or drop-in classroom visits, classify the behaviors you see based on the criteria on the card. Write these examples in the proper categories on the card.
- Dedicate a few minutes at each staff meeting to having an open conversation with staff members about a small number of criteria and how they are implemented in the classrooms. Jot down these examples.
- Meet with colleagues periodically to talk about the evaluation standards and share examples of their integration in classrooms.

THE ABILITY TO DESCRIBE DEFICIENT OR SUBSTANDARD WORK

This skill is essential in working with difficult or deficient teachers. If you can't clearly describe what is missing or what needs to be fixed in a lesson or classroom, it's pretty hard to tell the person exactly what she needs to do in order to improve and to develop the plan necessary to guide her through the process. Also, if the performance does not get better, you will have to give her the exact reasons why you are recommending termination. We have worked with many principals for whom this was a difficulty. In almost every case, those who could not clearly describe the deficits had a lot of trouble in eventually getting the teacher terminated. Here are some strategies that we have helped principals use in order to feel confident in identifying deficit performance areas with teachers:

- Read articles that describe effective teaching. Make notes of the effective strategies you see in these articles; compare these notes with what you see happening in the classroom of the deficient teacher.
- Watch other master teachers conduct their lessons, and notice the students' reactions when these teachers are implementing effective strategies. Compare the notes from this experience with what you see in the classrooms of those teachers you would consider deficient. Practice analyzing the gap between these two performances and what you think is missing from the ineffective instruction.
- Read books on effective teaching, and make notes of the strategies and ideas presented in them. As you watch instruction in classrooms where deficient performance is being exhibited, look for the gaps you see and think about what skills would need to be implemented in order to close those gaps.

As you spend time watching instruction, you will find it easier to quickly identify what needs to be put into place in order to improve the instruction.

BASE AND SURFACE COMPETENCIES

In Chapter 2, we introduced the concept of base and surface competencies (see Figure 2.1 for the blank reproducible template). Figure 5.1 is a sample of a completed template so you can see how you might use it with teachers.

Figure 5.1	Sample Completed Base and Surface Competencies Template for Teachers

Name Jane Smith   Job or Position Biology

Job Requirement/Competency	Base Competency	Surface Competency	Deficit Skill
Knowledge of content		X	X
Ability to explain content to students in a way that is understandable to them	X		X
Ability to empathize and understand student perspectives	X		
Ability to manage time to help make lessons efficient		X	
Ability to develop assessments matching student learning needs		X	X
Displays a caring attitude in working with children	X		

DECIDING WHETHER TO MOVE FORWARD TO TERMINATE EMPLOYMENT OR DEVELOP A GROWTH PLAN

After you have identified the deficiencies, you have to make a difficult decision. Do you think the teacher has the ability and desire to improve his performance if provided with a plan and guidance, or do you need to move to termination of this person's contract? This decision is one that only you can make and is normally based on a variety of factors. What should you take into account when making this decision? How will you know if you are making the correct decision?

Deciding whether to develop a growth plan and provide assistance for the teacher to improve or to move to termination is an individual decision based on the local conditions you face. However, there are some factors that we and others we have worked with over the years have used to make this difficult decision:

- *Severity of the deficiencies:* The decision to remediate or move to termination could be based on how bad things are in the classroom. Is the teacher way off base on the essential core teaching competencies? How far from competent is she? In your estimation, how long will it take for her to improve? The severity of the deficiencies needs to be taken into account when making a decision to remediate or terminate.

- *Number of areas in deficiency or needing improvement:* The decision to remediate or terminate should also be based on the number of areas that are deficient in the teacher's performance. We have found it difficult to help someone who has more than two to three deficiency areas. Because of the complexities associated with teaching and learning, it is hard to improve when there are a high number of needs in teaching performance.

- *Relationship between the deficiencies:* At times, the deficiencies you see when you evaluate a teacher are related. For example, he is unable to get students' attention at the beginning of a lesson, seems to run out of time, and has to rush at the end in order to provide the assignment. If the deficient areas are related, this teacher may be a candidate for a remediation plan. If the areas are completely different (e.g., the behavior management is deficient and the teacher is also doing a poor job assessing and using the results of the assessment to plan instruction), it may be difficult to remediate or help him. The degree of relationship between the deficient areas is something you will have to judge in making the decision to remediate or terminate employment.

- *Previous remediation attempts:* If you or someone else has tried to help the teacher improve but she keeps coming back to deficiency regularly, it may be time to move forward with termination. You have to make the decision, but repeated efforts to remediate should give you a clue that this teacher may not be able to learn and change. Use your judgment, and examine the situation carefully before moving forward.

- *Time required to teach this person the skills needed to become a better teacher:* Unless you have instructional coaches, curriculum specialists, and other resources available in your building to assist you in implementing the growth plan with a teacher, you will probably be doing the bulk of the work. Before you take on this responsibility, be sure to look at the time you have to devote to this project. Helping to remediate a teacher is time-consuming and difficult work. If you are involved in a remediation effort, you should try to reduce the other commitments you have so you don't get overwhelmed.

- *Your ability to teach this person the skills needed to become a better teacher:* If you are thinking about remediating the performance of a teacher, be sure to examine your knowledge and skills in the areas where you want the teacher to grow. You should be able to perform the skills you are asking him to implement and also be able to teach him how to improve. We have worked with embarrassed colleagues who tried to help a teacher improve, only to find out they couldn't do what they were asking the teacher to do, which helped the teacher justify part of his deficient behavior. You don't have to be a master at the skill, only able to explain and demonstrate it for the teacher.

- *Your administration and school board's attitude toward employee termination:* Be sure you find out what the administration and the school board think about termination before moving forward. Some administrators don't like the potential public outcry that can result from a termination. On the other hand, more and more district office staff, superintendents, and board members will support you if they feel that your recommendation is justified. Use this important aspect to help you make your decision about whether to remediate or move to termination.

- *Political realities in your community:* In some communities, there are teachers who have a lot of connections and political power. Think about this as you move forward with a deficient teacher. You never know who might be related or how deep the connections go. Many principals have taken on situations without thinking through this aspect and found themselves with a lot more conflict than they bargained for. We aren't saying that you should not take on highly connected teachers; you just need to think through the impacts before making a decision.

- *Physical and intellectual capacities of the teacher:* If the teacher you have identified as deficient does not possess common sense or is not able to learn, your remediation efforts will be very difficult. Some teachers have difficulties because they lack the basic intelligence to "get" what you are saying. Take the intellectual capacity of the person you are working with into account when making a termination or remediation decision.

- *Whether the deficiencies are base or surface competencies:* Remediating surface competencies is less complicated than remediating base competencies. Since base competencies develop over time and tend to be foundational in nature, they aren't as easily taught. Figure 5.1 will help you assess the base and surface competencies of teachers you work with who are not performing up to standards.

GROWTH PLANS

You will encounter employees that need a written growth plan in order to reinforce the severity of the problem and to provide them with a specific map to help them improve (see Figure 5.2 for a template). Figure 5.3 is a sample of a completed template for your reference.

Figure 5.2   Growth Plan Template

(INSERT SCHOOL NAME)
EMPLOYEE GROWTH PLAN

You are receiving this growth plan because serious concerns exist about your performance here at (insert school name). These concerns are summarized below:

- Name general behavior/performance problem #1
  Share specific examples of the problem
  - _____
  - _____

- Remind the teacher of previous times/instances when you addressed this behavior:
  - (List dates and anything you remember telling the employee)
  - (List dates and anything you remember telling the employee)
  - (List dates and anything you remember telling the employee)

- Share with the teacher why the issues you are bringing up are severe and need to be addressed:
  - Reason #1 _____
  - Reason #2 _____
  - Reason #3 _____

- Direct the teacher to stop the following behaviors/actions ("You are directed to immediately stop the following"):
  - List items here _____
  - List items here _____
  - List items here _____

If the inappropriate behavior does not stop immediately, further disciplinary action can occur, up to and including termination of employment.
I understand and agree to the terms of this plan.

_____   _____

Employee signature   Supervisor signature

Figure 5.3   Sample Completed Growth Plan for Teachers

(INSERT SCHOOL NAME)
EMPLOYEE GROWTH PLAN

You are receiving this growth plan because serious concerns exist about your performance here at (insert school name). These concerns are summarized below:

- Your ability to relate to the students. During several lessons that I have observed this year, you have had a hard time relating to the students. I've seen you argue with them, use inappropriate sarcasm, and put students down in front of their peers. This is not the first time we have talked about this problem:
  - On September 15, I was observing in your room when I saw you put down three students. I immediately spoke with you after the lesson and shared my concern with your behavior. You said you would monitor it.
  - On September 20, I was doing some walk-through visits when I saw a similar incident except with the use of sarcasm. When I met with you to talk about my concern, you said that the student knew you were kidding and that the sarcasm was OK. I told you that I wasn't OK with it and that I had noticed that the student looked upset. I told you to avoid the use of sarcasm in your room in the future.
  - On October 3, I saw you put down several students during your class. In the conference that followed that incident, I told you the behavior must stop immediately or I would set up a meeting to develop a more formal plan.

- Treating students the way that I've seen you treat them, and which I have addressed in my conferences, is a problem. Here are a few reasons why:
  - When you put students down, you set a very negative tone in your classroom. This gets in the way of student learning and success.
  - Your put-downs and sarcasm set a poor example for your students. You need to serve as a role model for their behaviors.

- In the past I have shared strategies to help you monitor and stop this behavior. Here are some ideas for you to consider in addressing this behavior:
  - Observe in other classrooms and look for how these teachers build connections with students.
  - Record the introductory part of your class. Listen to it, and identify when you are beginning to get sarcastic or use put-downs. Once you can monitor the situation, you can begin to develop strategies to address it.
  - I will be happy to model a lesson for you or observe you in class to give you informal feedback on your efforts to improve your relationships with students.

You need to immediately stop putting down students, belittling them, and using sarcasm in your classroom. If the inappropriate behavior does not stop immediately, further disciplinary action can occur, up to and including termination of employment. I understand and agree to the terms of this plan.

_____   _____
Employee signature   Supervisor signature

DELIVERING A DEFICIENCY NOTICE OR TERMINATION MESSAGE TO A TEACHER

Obviously, the rubber meets the road when it comes time to actually sit down with a teacher and deliver the message that his performance is deficient, that you are putting him on a growth plan, or that you are recommending that his contract be terminated. We have found it helpful to script the entire conference to ensure that you stay focused and on track. Figure 5.4 is a template that you can use to script your conference with a teacher.

Figure 5.4	Template for Delivering a Deficiency Notice or Termination Message to a Teacher

Set a professional tone

In this phase of the conference, the supervisor opens the conference and lets the teacher know that it will be a professional experience. *Example statement: Thank you for coming in today to talk about your performance review.*

(Your planned opening here)

_____

_____

_____

_____

_____

Provide an overview of the conferencing process

People like it when they know what is coming up. Use this phase of the conference to lay out the plan for your time with the teacher. *Example statement: During this conference, I plan to share your summative evaluation with you. I also plan to let you know how you are doing in relation to division expectations.*

(Your planned overview here)

_____

_____

_____

_____

_____

Reinforce any effective performance areas

In this section, you can give the teacher feedback about any performance areas that are meeting division standards. Be careful in reinforcing any areas that may be related to the deficient areas you will be talking about later in the conference. *Example statement: Throughout the school year, I have noticed that you have tried hard to get to know the* students. You have also. . . . These behaviors fit under Performance Area 3, the classroom environment.

(Your planned reinforcement comments here)

_____

_____

_____

_____

_____

Define deficient performance areas

In this phase of the conference, clearly define what is deficient about the teacher's overall performance and why it is deficient. *Example statement: Throughout the year, we have talked about your performance in the areas of instruction and classroom management. In spite of your efforts, these areas are still not meeting division standards. I will be recommending that your contract not be renewed. I'll be giving you more information about your specific performance in these areas in a few minutes.*

(Your discussion of deficiencies here)

_____

_____

_____

_____

_____

Give clear, clean examples of deficiency

Be sure to provide clear examples from the observations and other data courses where the deficiency or deficiencies are occurring. *Example statement: Throughout the school year, we have been talking about concerns I have had in the areas of . . . (cite examples from various lessons throughout the year).*

(Your examples here)

_____

_____

_____

_____

_____

Restate why this behavior is an issue and that the performance is not meeting school standards

At this point you may think that what you have covered is very clear, but you need to sum up all of the information you just presented and remind the employee that he or she is not meeting standards. You need to let the employee know that if the behavior does not improve you will be recommending termination. *First example statement (which would be used in cases where the deficiencies may lead to termination): All of the deficiencies I just mentioned have contributed to my decision that you are not meeting division standards, and therefore I will not recommend that your contract be renewed. Second example statement (which would be used in cases where the*

(Continued)

Figure 5.4   (Continued)

deficiencies may lead to the development and implementation of a growth plan): At this point in the evaluation process, you are not meeting district standards. Your deficiencies in these areas are serious enough that I need to work with you to develop a growth plan.

(Your conclusions here)

_____

_____

_____

_____

_____

Share strategies for improvement and outline your follow-up plan for supporting the employee

Talk to the teacher about what he or she can do to respond to the evaluation, the next steps in the process, and any other rights he or she has in relation to the evaluation. *Example statement: You can write a response to my evaluation. You need to submit a response to me by (date). If you give me a response, I will attach it to my copy. You also have the right to a hearing with the superintendent. If you are interested in a hearing, you need to contact her office by (date). If you want to have representation with you at this meeting, you can . . . (provide more details).*

(Your strategies and plan here)

_____

_____

_____

_____

_____

Thank the employee for meeting with you. Let the employee know when a summary of this conference will be ready for his or her signature and whether any other paperwork will be delivered.

Even though this can be a tense meeting, you want to treat the employee with respect (no matter how he or she reacts) so that the meeting stays professional. *Example statement: I know this has been a stressful meeting, but I appreciate you giving me your time and listening as I shared your evaluation. I will have a summary of this conference typed up and ready for your signature by tomorrow. There will be other paperwork from the superintendent's office delivered here by . . . (date).*

(Your closing comments here)

_____

_____

_____

_____

_____

Here is an example of how these difficult conferences may sound with real deficient teacher behaviors:

| Melanie (the principal): | Sharon, thank you for meeting with me today. I appreciate your professionalism as we continue to work together to improve your teaching. Let me share an overview of our meeting today. First, I want to update you on the status of your progress on the teacher evaluation process that we have been working on throughout the year. Second, I want to get your perceptions about your performance. Finally, I'd like to share my plans for working with you for the remainder of the year.

Let's get started. We have been working to improve your classroom management. I have personally made five visits to your classroom and provided you with ideas and strategies that you could implement. I have also connected you with two other teachers in the building and provided substitutes for you so you can observe these teachers' classrooms to see how they manage their students. After that and some of the other strategies we have implemented, you are still not meeting the district standards for classroom management. I still see the students misbehaving in your classroom. They are still sending and receiving text messages, talking with each other, and passing notes. Even when you stop teaching to deal with their misbehaviors, they ignore you and go on with their own agendas. Your repeated directions to them are ignored. As a result of that, I am placing you on intensive assistance for the remainder of the year. |
|---|---|
| Sharon (the teacher): | I am shocked by your assessment. I feel I have made good progress toward improving my classroom management. I disagree with your conclusion and don't feel I need to be on intensive assistance. I can improve on my own. |
| Melanie: | Thanks for sharing your perspective on your growth. I agree that you have made some growth, just not enough to alleviate my concerns. Being involved in the intensive assistance process has the potential to help you improve your teaching in the areas of concern. You have the right to provide a rebuttal to my assessment and even refuse to take advantage of the intensive assessment process. I hope you choose to take advantage of the intensive assistance process, but if you refuse it, you will go on the regular evaluation process and won't have access to some of the resources available from the intensive assistance. After we finish our meeting, you have three days to submit your reply to my evaluation report. You also have the right to ask the assistant superintendent to review your situation and provide her perspective. Again, please let me know how you want to proceed after we finish our conference today. |

Sharon: I don't agree with you, and I will be providing a rebuttal to your evaluation. I will let you know what else I plan to do after I see your conference summary.

Melanie: Thank you. I will have the conference summary ready for you to review by the end of the day tomorrow. I will personally bring it to your classroom so you can see it right away. Be sure to use the space at the bottom of the form or attach your own letter or memo to the conference summary.

As you can see from this brief summary of their interaction, there was no agreement between Sharon and Melanie. Even though a high level of conflict existed in the meeting, Melanie, the principal, stayed on track and delivered her message to Sharon. Sharon tried to take her off track with her challenge, but Melanie followed her script, stayed calm, and delivered her message.

THE ENTIRE CYCLE

We have designed the following examples that take you through the entire cycle of dealing with difficult or deficient employees. They include a brief overview of the situation, a summary of the meeting held to address the concerns, and written summaries used for follow-up with the teacher.

Cindy, a principal at a middle school, has been having difficulty with a teacher who treats students in a demeaning and insensitive manner such as yelling and using inappropriate language and ignoring directives concerning the medical conditions of students. On several occasions, Cindy met with the teacher to have a conversation about specific incidents that she observed or that other staff members, students, and parents had reported to her. The teacher denied that the incidents occurred. He told Cindy that he is just joking around with the students and that they take him too seriously. The teacher stated, "I am trying to relate to the students by using humor in my classroom." Cindy asked him why he denied permission for a student to go to the nurse's office for her medication. The teacher informed Cindy that the student lied and had never asked to go to the nurse's office.

Cindy decided that since the teacher was uncooperative, denied the incidents, and refused to make the necessary changes, it was best to give him a letter of reprimand and a plan for assistance.

Cindy told the teacher that she wanted to meet with him again and that he could have a union representative present at the meeting. (When you are requesting to meet with a teacher, it is important to put the information in writing and to give the letter to the teacher at least 24 to 48 hours prior to the meeting time.)

Here is an example of the letter used to inform the teacher of the upcoming meeting:

Date
To: Teacher name
From: Principal
Re: Meeting

This is to verify that I request a meeting with you on (date) at (time) in my office at (school name).

You have the right to have union representation present at the meeting if you choose to do so.

Sincerely,

Principal

At the meeting, Cindy gave the teacher the following letter of reprimand and presented specific directives:

Date

Teacher name

Re: Letter of Reprimand and Plan of Assistance

This is a formal letter of reprimand. Failure to follow the directives in this letter may be grounds for additional discipline up to and including termination. (Teacher name) is reprimanded for inappropriate conduct toward students, specifically treating students in a demeaning and insensitive manner, using inappropriate language, and ignoring directives concerning students' medical conditions.

(In the next part of the letter, you could add specific recommendations. Listed below are some examples:

- *You are directed to treat students in a respectful manner.*
- *You are directed to allow children with a medical condition to go to the nurse's office if they request to do so.*
- *You are directed to refrain from using inappropriate language with students.)*

If you have any questions about these directives, please contact your supervisor for clarification. Your supervisor will review these directives at the end of the school year.

Sincerely,

Principal or supervisor

cc: Personnel file

If you observe that the teacher does not follow the directives you provided in the meeting and in the first follow-up letter, it is important to hold another meeting to increase the accountability and further highlight the consequences. Here is a letter that could be used:

Date

Teacher

Re: Follow-up Meeting Regarding the Letter of Reprimand

This is to formally notify you that I would like to meet with you to follow up on the letter of reprimand that was given to you on (date you gave the letter).
The meeting will be held on (date) at (time) in (location).
The purpose of the meeting will be to give you a short update on your progress in meeting the directives given to you in the (date) letter as well as to discuss the letter of reprimand.
This letter allows you (time according to the contract, such as 24 hours) to obtain union representation for the meeting as required by the master contract. If you have questions, please contact me.

Sincerely,

Principal

In the following example, the principal addresses a situation in which a teacher uses excessive physical force in dealing with a student.

Mike, a middle school principal, learned that a teacher had used physical force during a physical education class in order to make a student comply with his directives when the student refused to listen to him. This incident was reported to Mike by another staff member. Mike felt it was important to take immediate action. He did not want a staff member using force to make a student follow directions. Mike first interviewed the teacher who reported the incident, and then he interviewed the student in question and other students who witnessed the incident. Then Mike felt that it was important to interview the teacher about using physical force with a student during physical education class.

Mike informed the teacher that he wanted to meet with him about the incident during his physical education class. At the meeting, Mike gave the teacher a Tennessean Warning (see the following example), which is used to inform an employee that he will be asked questions and that the answers may be used in disciplinary actions against that employee.

During the course of this interview, I will be asking you questions. You do not have to answer any of my questions. If you do not answer my questions or provide me with information, (name the school district) will have to make its decision regarding our concerns without your input.

The information you give me during this interview may be shared with school district personnel who need to know, which may include the director of administrative services, the superintendent, school board members, and any other individuals directly or indirectly involved in the matters discussed.

_____   _____

Teacher's signature   Supervisor's signature

Mike interviewed the teacher and found out during the interview that the teacher did use physical force with the student. During the interview, Mike made sure he documented everything the teacher said.

After the meeting, Mike felt that it was important to give the teacher a letter of direction (see the following two examples).

Date

Teacher's Name
Teacher's assignment

This is a letter of direction setting forth behavior concerns that require your immediate correction.

On (date) you used physical force to make a child comply with your directives during physical education class when he refused to follow your directions, and you spoke to the students in a manner that was inappropriate and disrespectful.

You are directed as follows:

1. Do not use physical force with students. At no time are you to use physical force in order to force students to move or to comply with your directives when they are resisting.

2. At all times, speak and act in a respectful and professional manner with district staff, students, and parents. Disrespectful language or behavior will not be tolerated.

Failure to correct these issues and comply with these directives immediately will result in discipline, up to and including termination.

In addition, you may not discuss, comment, or make remarks regarding this letter, the directives included in this letter, or your private personnel issues with anyone other than your supervisor and union representative during your workday. You may not retaliate against any individuals, directly or indirectly, whom you believe were involved in the school district's investigation of your conduct. Retaliatory behavior will lead to discipline.

Sincerely,

Principal

cc: Personnel File

Date

Teacher name

This is a letter of direction setting forth expectations as a result of an incident that occurred at (name of school) on (date of incident) in which you used physical force to make a student comply with your directives.

1. At no time are you to use physical force to make students move or comply with your directives when they are resisting.

2. You are to immediately contact the building principal any time you have a student who repeatedly refuses to cooperate.

If you have any questions, please feel free to contact me.

Sincerely,

Principal

In both of these cases, the written notice was used to reinforce the conference that was held and to communicate the severity of the situation.

SUMMARY

We spend most of our time and attention working with and evaluating teachers. In this chapter, we have outlined some ideas that will be helpful to you as you work with difficult teachers. As you reflect on the information in this chapter, consider the following questions:

- What are some of the factors you need to consider when making a decision to remediate or move forward with termination of a deficient teacher?
- What purpose does a letter of deficiency serve? What kind of information might need to be considered when writing such a letter?
- As you think about developing a conference for a marginal or deficient teacher, what components should you consider?
- Why is it important to understand the concepts of surface and base competencies when working with marginal or deficient teachers?

Even though working with marginal or deficient teachers is complex, the strategies presented in this chapter will give you support and guidance as you take on these difficult school employees. In Chapter 6, you will learn ideas and techniques for dealing with administrative assistants and office staff. When your office staff is substandard or deficient, it impacts your effectiveness as the building administrator. Chapter 6 will help you get a handle on this employee group.

NOTES

Write any notes that you think might be helpful to you as you implement the strategies/ideas presented in this chapter with your difficult employees. Feel free to refer back to these notes as you need to when confronting their issues or behaviors.

_____

_____

_____

_____

_____

_____

_____

_____

_____

_____

_____

_____

_____

_____

_____

6

Strategies for Working With Difficult/Marginal Administrative Assistants and Office Staff

T he staff that works in your office is a direct reflection of your organization and of your leadership priorities and abilities. A good office staff member can make you shine, whereas a bad employee can make you look bad. Effective leaders work to build the kind of office staff that reflects the goals of the operation, provides exceptional customer service, and maintains confidentiality. What do great leaders do to address those staff members that are deficient? We will explore those strategies in this chapter. In this chapter you will learn about the following:

- understanding the basic mode of operation of office staff members
- clearly communicating to office staff your expectations for performance and customer interactions
- assessing your office for areas or situations that need to be addressed
- developing an improvement plan for deficient office staff members
- documenting performance issues related to office staff operation

- delivering improvement conferences to staff members who do not meet expectations
- assessing improvement in performance and making decisions related to improvement based on job standards
- examining common areas of concern in offices and the strategies to deal with these concerns
- successfully making a case for termination of deficient office staff members

HANDLING YOUR ADMINISTRATIVE ASSISTANTS

Administrative assistants are pivotal to the success of a school. When you have a great administrative assistant, your school runs well; when this person's performance is poor, your school does not run well. Let's see how Bill, an elementary school principal, handles an administrative assistant with a very common difficult problem:

Bill suspects that his administrative assistant, Jane, is talking negatively about the school to parents. He has noticed that her voice sometimes gets lower when he comes into the office. He has been told by several parents that Jane has told them negative things about the school. And faculty members have made comments about Jane's negative comments. Since Bill only suspects her negative behaviors, he decides to conduct an investigation. Over a period of several weeks, he picks up information that confirms his suspicions.

Once Bill confirms his suspicions, he decides to confront Jane's behavior. He lists specific problems that he has with her behavior and job performance, and he uses this information to design a conference in which he will confront her problems and establish a plan for her to improve. His conference includes the following components:

- setting a professional tone for the conference and letting Jane know he wants to talk with her about a concern related to her performance
- providing specific information about the exact issues he has with her performance
- providing specific examples of the behaviors that contribute to her performance issues
- making sure he knows that she understands what he is concerned about and what he wants her to improve on
- providing specific strategies that he will use to follow up with her and keep her on track

Bill sets up a meeting with Jane and implements his conference plan. As expected, she spends time and energy trying to deny the behavior and makes excuses for what Bill had found. He gets her back on track several times using framing and moves her through the conference. He works with Jane to design a plan to help her appropriately deal with her concerns rather than involve outsiders in her issues. Bill keeps a close watch on her for the next year and notices that the strategies they developed appear to be working. But he has to be prepared to move to termination in the event that Jane cannot eliminate the problem.

In this example, the resolution turned out to be relatively positive. Not every situation ends up like this. Bill was working on solid ground when he confronted Jane because he had done his homework to research the issue and put in the time to design and implement a conference to confront Jane about her behavior. By being organized and confronting issues with your administrative assistant, you can either improve the behavior or move toward termination.

Here are some of the difficult behaviors we have dealt with in regard to administrative assistants:

- staying too late and then asking for overtime
- being unfriendly to parents and students
- talking on the phone doing nonschool business
- running a business at school
- having poor organization or task completion skills
- having unclean or disorganized office space
- trying to be the unofficial principal of the school
- gossiping or talking negatively about others
- undermining the principal with other staff members

A BASIC SET OF ADMINISTRATIVE ASSISTANT/OFFICE EMPLOYEE TASKS

While the roles and responsibilities of administrative assistants are varied, the list in Figure 6.1 includes some common components that are associated with effective office operations. These elements are also some of the most common that we dealt with in our work in schools over the years. Use this list to make a preliminary assessment of your office staff and operations.

BASE AND SURFACE COMPETENCIES

When getting ready to confront administrative assistants, it's important to identify the skills in deficit. In Chapter 2, we introduced a template to help you identify the base and surface competencies possessed by the various

Figure 6.1   Office Operations Checklist

This is a partial list of the functions that are typically important to the operation of an office. Use the template to assess and evaluate your office operations and begin to develop a plan for addressing any deficiencies. You should come up with your own standards for the columns measuring performance since office effectiveness is locally determined.

Office Component	Desired Level of Performance	Satisfactory Level of Performance	Unsatisfactory Level of Performance
Meeting and welcoming visitors			
Handling phone calls from staff, parents, community members, salespeople, and the media			
Procedures for parents and students to visit the school			
Visitor sign-in and badge procedures			
Office hours defined and posted			
Procedures for the office staff related to volunteers in the school			
Welcome packets and other information sources for new families			
Procedures for scheduling appointments and meetings, and meetings with the principal			
Establishing and maintaining a professional office atmosphere			

(Continued)

Figure 6.1	(Continued)

Office Component	Desired Level of Performance	Satisfactory Level of Performance	Unsatisfactory Level of Performance
Handling confidential or potentially sensitive information			
Managing forms for staff, parents, and students			
Procedures for the office related to fire drills, tornado drills, and lockdowns			
Procedures for the office related to phone calls to teachers/classrooms			
Procedures for the office related to communication with parents and community members			
Posting a school calendar of events such as field trips, meetings, and when the building is in use			
Procedures to keep office staff current on office tasks, such as in the area of technology, building security, and staff development training			
Procedures to keep office informed on building goals, initiatives, and programs			
Other, as needed			

Source: Adapted from Eller & Eller, 2009.

employees you supervise (see Figure 2.1 for the blank reproducible template). Figure 6.2 is a sample of a completed template so you can see how you might use it with your office staff. As we mentioned earlier, base and surface competencies are important for you to plot because knowing them will help you determine the severity of any skill deficits and the relative difficulty you may face in trying to remediate the performance of your employees. Remember, base competencies are more complicated to remediate than surface competencies. Keep this in mind as you consider remediation or possible termination for your office staff.

Figure 6.2	Sample Completed Base and Surface Competencies Template for Administrative Assistants and Office Staff

Name Kim Long Job or Position Administrative Assistant			
Job Requirement/ Competency	Base Competency	Surface Competency	Deficit Skill
Ability to use various software packages to manage office operations		X	
Ability to prioritize the principal's schedule based on the day's demands	X		X
Ability to organize files in a manner that makes information easy to find		X	X
Ability to meet and greet clients and make them feel comfortable	X		
Ability to manage the school budget process		X	
Ability to talk with and calm down an angry parent	X		

PRIORITIZING WORK TASKS

One way of helping staff members effectively fulfill the most important parts of their jobs is to assist them in setting priorities for work completion for an upcoming period of time. We have found it helpful to look at three priority areas:

- *Priority 1:* These are tasks that are required for the safe and continued operation of the school:
  - o student safety information notifications

- o short-term parent notifications for their children related to schedule changes
- o immediate district informational needs
- o immediate information needs for the superintendent
- o parents' messages and appointments for the principal
- o scheduling planning and prioritizing meetings between the principal and the administrative assistant
- *Priority 2:* These are tasks that are important but have longer-range implications:
  - o regular district and state-level informational reports
  - o regular parent and community informational reports such as newsletters
  - o regular material and supply orders
- *Priority 3:* These tasks tend to be less important for the day-to-day operation of the school but have long-range implications:
  - o scheduling regular and reoccurring events

At the beginning of the week, it's important to first schedule the Priority 1 items, followed by the Priority 2 and 3 items. There should be only a few Priority 1 items on the schedule since they tend to take the most time in their implementation. A weekly schedule might look like this:

Monday	Tuesday	Wednesday	Thursday	Friday
• Priority 1 task • Three Priority 2 tasks	• Priority 1 task			

PLANNING SESSIONS TO ESTABLISH PRIORITIES FOR THE WORK COMPLETION

A strategy that works well with all administrative assistants, but especially helps you more closely supervise a difficult or deficient one, is to establish and follow through on a weekly goal-setting/planning meeting. This not only keeps the two of you in sync but also helps you closely monitor the workload and production schedule. We established the schedule in Figure 6.3 for our planning meetings:

Regular planning and the ability to monitor and adjust based on changing needs can help as you encounter changes and unanticipated challenges during the week. It also helps to keep difficult/marginal administrative assistants focused and productive because it provides a clear structure for them to use in organizing their workload. By conducting regular meetings, you help them reprioritize what needs to be done.

Figure 6.3 Sample Planning and Prioritizing Meeting Schedule

Week	Monday	Tuesday	Wednesday	Thursday	Friday
1					• Review the previous week's tasks and accomplishments • Establish preliminary goals and priorities for the upcoming week
2	• Implement plan	• Meet to review the progress on established goals and priorities • Establish refined goals/priorities	• Implement plan	• Implement plan	• Review the previous week's tasks and accomplishments • Establish preliminary goals and priorities for the upcoming week
3	• Implement plan	• Meet to review the progress on established goals and priorities • Establish refined goals/priorities	• Implement plan	• Implement plan	• Review the previous week's tasks and accomplishments • Establish preliminary goals and priorities for the upcoming week
4	• Implement plan	• Meet to review the progress on established goals and priorities • Establish refined goals/priorities	• Implement plan	• Implement plan	• Review the previous week's tasks and accomplishments • Establish preliminary goals and priorities for the upcoming week

GROWTH PLANS

When working with administrative assistants, you may need to move beyond the verbal meeting to a written reprimand or directive. Figure 6.4 is a sample of a completed growth plan to help you get an idea of how one might be developed for an employee. (See Figure 5.2 for the blank reproducible version of the template.)

| Figure 6.4 | Sample Completed Growth Plan for Administrative Assistants and Office Staff |

(INSERT SCHOOL NAME)
EMPLOYEE GROWTH PLAN

You are receiving this growth plan because serious concerns exist about your performance here at (insert school name). These concerns are summarized below:

- Your attitude and demeanor when working with parents. Over the past six months, I have observed you treating parents in a negative manner. You have raised your voice when asked questions, rolled your eyes when you see certain parents enter the office, told parents that you are too busy to help them, and turned away and pretended to be busy when certain parents entered the office.

- Your attitude and demeanor when working with teachers and staff members. During the same period of time, I have also observed you treat staff members in a negative manner. When staff members have asked you for paperwork, you comment that you are too busy and that they should come back later. You have also raised your voice with certain staff members and even started to argue with some of them when they shared ideas with you.

- This information is not new to you. I have talked to you repeatedly over the past six months to let you know my concerns with this behavior:

  o On October 14, I spoke with you about my concern after an incident in which you raised your voice to Mrs. Smith. She came to me shortly afterward, and I met with you immediately to share my concern with this behavior. I told you to control your temper when working with parents and gave you some ideas to help you when you feel frustrated. You thanked me for the ideas and said they would be helpful to you.

  o On October 27, one of the staff members reported having an altercation with you. Again, I met with you and we talked about strategies to use to avoid these kinds of situations in the future. You said you knew what you needed to do in order to avoid a problem.

  o On February 25, I spoke with you again about a series of incidents in which you lost your temper with parents and staff. Again, we talked about why this issue is so important and you said you would keep it under control in the future. I shared that if the behavior continues we would have to meet and develop a formal plan.

- I will repeat here what I've told you related to why this behavior is a problem:
  - In the office, you set the tone for the entire school. When you are negative, it communicates that our school is negative.
  - Most people who come into our office are looking for good customer service. Your behavior does not exhibit the kind of customer service that we want to provide to our stakeholders.
  - Finally, once you upset others, it takes a lot of time and work for the rest of us to calm them down and develop a good working relationship.

- As we have verbally discussed in the past, your negative attitude and behaviors are inappropriate. You are directed to immediately stop doing the following:
  - Raising your voice with parents and staff members
  - Treating parents and staff members in a negative manner
  - Telling staff members that you are too busy to appropriately help them when asked

I plan to check in with you on a weekly basis to see how things are going. I will be happy to help you with any ideas or strategies that you may need in order to be successful. I will also work with you to temporarily avoid intense interactions with some of the more difficult parents until you feel comfortable with your new skills. If the inappropriate behavior does not stop immediately, further disciplinary action can occur, up to and including termination of employment.

I understand and agree to the terms of this plan.

_____   _____

Employee signature   Supervisor signature

DELIVERING A DEFICIENCY NOTICE OR TERMINATION MESSAGE TO AN ADMINISTRATIVE ASSISTANT

As we mentioned in Chapter 5, there comes a time when you need to sit down with a marginal or deficient employee and provide directives for improvement. Just like the teacher conference outlined earlier, the growth or termination conference for an administrative assistant has several phases. We kept the phases the same for all employee groups so that you could learn and remember one general conferencing template (see Figure 6.5). Once you have this mastered, you can then add specifics related to the employees you are supervising.

Figure 6.5	Template for Delivering a Deficiency Notice or Termination Message to an Administrative Assistant

Set a professional tone

In this phase of the conference, the supervisor opens the conference and lets the administrative assistant know that it will be a professional experience. *Example statement: Thank you for meeting with me. I need to talk to you about a concern I have.*

(Your planned opening here)

_____

_____

_____

_____

_____

Provide an overview of the conferencing process

People like it when they know what is coming up. Use this phase of the conference to lay out the plan for your time with the administrative assistant. *Example statement: During this conference, I'll share my concerns related to your performance and give you specific examples of what I mean.*

(Your planned overview here)

_____

_____

_____

_____

_____

Define deficient performance areas

In this phase of the conference, clearly define what is deficient about the administrative assistant's overall performance and why it is deficient. *Example statement: I have a concern about how you talk to people who call the school. When people call, you are very short and curt with them. From my observations, it sounds like you are annoyed when people call. Next, I'll be giving you more information about your specific performance in these areas.*

(Your discussion of deficiencies here)

_____

_____

_____

_____

_____

Give clear, clean examples of deficiency

Be sure to provide clear examples from the observations and other data courses where the deficiency or deficiencies are occurring. *Example statement: On March 4, I overheard you lecturing a caller for asking a question. On March 15, I heard you raise your voice when a parent seemed to not understand your response. Finally, on April 11, you told a parent that you would not give a message to her child about a change in the child's afterschool care plans. In general, whenever you answer the phone you sound grumpy and do not ask parents how you can help them as we agreed in an earlier conference.*

(Your examples here)

_____

_____

_____

_____

_____

Restate why this behavior is an issue and that the performance is not meeting the school standards

At this point you may think that what you have covered is very clear, but you need to sum up all of the information you just presented and remind the employee that he or she is not meeting standards. You need to let the employee know if the behavior does not improve

Figure 6.5 (Continued)

you will be recommending termination. *First example statement (which would be used in cases where the deficiencies may lead to termination): When you don't answer the phone in a welcoming manner, it turns off the callers or makes them more hostile for others to deal with later. It sets a bad tone or reputation for our school. If this behavior cannot be addressed, I may need to move to terminate your employment, but I'm sure we can work things out. Second example statement (which would be used if you plan to develop an improvement plan): At this point, I have concerns about your performance. I will work with you to develop an improvement plan to address these issues.*

(Your conclusions here)

_____

_____

_____

_____

_____

Share strategies for improvement and outline your follow-up plan for supporting the employee

Talk to the administrative assistant about what he or she can do to respond to the evaluation, the next steps in the process, and any other rights he or she has in relation to the evaluation. *Example statement: Here is what you need to do in order to change your behavior (share specific plan and strategies). I will check in with you in a few days to see how you are doing. It is my expectation that your efforts should be able to address my concerns. (You can also outline a more detailed improvement plan if you are able and see a need.)*

(Your strategies and plan here)

_____

_____

_____

_____

_____

SUMMARY

Administrative assistants and office staff can be a direct reflection of the competence of the administrator that supervises them. Since they are so important to the success of a school, it is important for you to be able to work with them to ensure that they are competent and are portraying the desired image of your school. In this chapter, we have provided you with ideas and insights about how you can effectively work with administrative assistants and office staff to ensure a positive image. As you reflect on the major content in this chapter, think about the following:

- What skills and competencies are crucial for the operation of your office?
- How do the concepts of base and surface competencies impact your ability to influence and change the behaviors of your administrative assistants and office staff?
- What are the key components that need to be included in a performance improvement conference? How do you plan and deliver this type of conference to your administrative assistants and office staff?

As you move forward in your efforts to improve your office staff, keep the ideas and strategies you learned in previous chapters in mind as well.

NOTES

Write any notes that you think might be helpful to you as you implement the strategies/ideas presented in this chapter with your difficult employees. Feel free to refer back to these notes as you need to when confronting their issues or behaviors.

_____

_____

_____

_____

_____

_____

_____

_____

_____

_____

_____

_____

_____

_____

7

Strategies for Working With Difficult/Marginal Paraprofessionals and Teaching Assistants

Instructional paraprofessionals, assistants, and aides are used in virtually every school in the country. These professionals provide students and teachers with great support in most cases, but occasionally their performance falls far short of expectations. In these cases, you may need to address the concerns and either help them improve or remove them from the educational setting. In this chapter, we will highlight strategies and techniques for successfully working with difficult/deficient paraprofessionals and teaching assistants. As you work through the information in this chapter, you will learn about the following:

- understanding the basic mode of operation of paraprofessionals and teaching assistants
- developing an improvement plan for deficient paraprofessionals and teaching assistants
- delivering improvement conferences to staff members who are not meeting expectations
- successfully making a case for termination of deficient paraprofessionals and teaching assistants

Tony, a high school principal, had a paraprofessional, Shelly, working in a special needs program. Several students reported to Tony that she was making derogatory statements to the some of the children. He immediately decided to investigate the situation. Several program teachers also said that they overheard Shelly making negative comments to her students. When Tony conducted formal interviews with the students in the program and was told that Shelly had made comments to them like "Why can't you get this?" or "What is wrong with you?" he knew he was facing a very serious problem. He knew he had to take action to protect the children and deal with this situation.

In response to this situation, Tony took these steps:

- conduct a thorough and fair investigation related to the allegations
- meet with the paraprofessional in question to make her aware of the situation
- take action related to the allegations and the results of the investigation

THE NATURE OF TEACHING ASSISTANTS AND PARAPROFESSIONALS

It's easy to typecast or stereotype people into classifications, but over the years we have found that most teaching assistants and paraprofessionals have certain characteristics. Knowing or learning these can help you better understand and work with this employee group. Here are some of the more common characteristics we have found, which are important to keep in mind as you supervise these employees:

- *Members of the community:* Many of the paraprofessionals we have worked with are people who live in the community, whereas a large number of the teachers we have worked with do not. Coming from the community can give paraprofessionals a slightly different outlook since they may see some of the students and parents outside of school, pay local taxes, and be significantly invested in the success of the community.
- *Very loyal:* Paraprofessionals and teaching assistants tend to be very loyal to the school, the students, and their teachers. Sometimes their loyalty causes them to cover for or defend the actions of others.
- *At one or the other end of a vast spectrum:* Most paraprofessionals and teaching assistants are coming to this position either right out of college or with lots of experience. This reality poses entirely different supervision challenges. Brand-new paraprofessionals may lack in strategies and ideas and may be trying to build their skills in order

to become teachers. On the other hand, those who have lots of experience may have already raised several children (and a few teachers and principals); these people have been around the block and may present challenges to supervisors because they could be resistant to change or taking direction.

- *Have been made to feel less important than other staff members:* You may not have done it, and nobody presently at the school may have done it, but at some time someone said or did something to make your paraprofessionals feel less important than other staff members. This feeling can cause people to resent and resist comments designed to redirect them. Some may even take your redirection as a put-down. Think and act carefully and respectfully when providing directives to paraprofessionals and teaching assistants.
- *Tend to do specialized jobs:* When paraprofessionals are assigned a job, it is normally highly specialized. They can get very good at doing the specialized job and may be resistant to redirection. You may want to take time to get to know them and the nature of the job that they do before giving advice.
- *Follow through on plans made by a teacher:* Since most paraprofessionals work at the direction of a teacher, they normally have clear assignments. Keep this in mind and check with the teacher first before providing a redirection of a paraprofessional's assignment or the strategies used in completing the assignment.

BASE AND SURFACE COMPETENCIES

When getting ready to confront paraprofessionals, it's important to identify the skills in deficit. In Chapter 2, we introduced a template to help you identify the foundational and technical skills possessed by the various employees you supervise. We include a completed sample of that template in Figure 7.1 to help you see how one might identify the foundational and technical skills of an employee.

GROWTH PLANS

At times, you will need to issue written directives to your employees that let them know they need to stop engaging in a particular behavior and get themselves back on track. As with any directive, you need to meet with the employee and be clear and specific as you deliver the message. Figure 7.2 is a sample of a completed growth plan to help you get an idea of how one might be developed for an employee. (See Figure 5.2 for the blank reproducible version of the template.)

| Figure 7.1 | Sample Completed Base and Surface Competencies Template for Paraprofessionals and Teaching Assistants |

Name <u>Anne Jones</u>   Job or Position <u>Classroom Paraprofessional</u>

Job Requirement/ Competency	Base Competency	Surface Competency	Deficit Skill
Ability to take direction from a classroom teacher	X		
Ability to communicate with the teacher about student needs		X	
Ability to build rapport and work with a student successfully	X		
Ability to organize instructional space		X	
Ability to write summaries of instructional sessions		X	

| Figure 7.2 | Sample Completed Growth Plan for Paraprofessionals and Teaching Assistants |

(INSERT SCHOOL NAME)
EMPLOYEE GROWTH PLAN

You are receiving this growth plan because serious concerns exist about your performance here at (insert school name). These concerns are summarized below:

- Your relationships with students at (insert school name) are inappropriate. In general, the inappropriate relationships revolve around the negative comments you make to the students in your class. Specific examples of these inappropriate interactions include:
  - On September 15, you said to one student, "Why are you so stupid?"
  - On September 17, you said to a student, "What were you thinking? Obviously you weren't using your head on that one."
  - On October 20, you said to a group of students as they entered the classroom, "Here come the geniuses again." This was obviously meant to belittle them.

(Continued)

Figure 7.2 (Continued)

- You have received verbal reminders and warnings on the following dates that these interactions were inappropriate:
  - After each of the incidents, I reminded you why your comments were inappropriate and how they potentially hurt the students' feelings.

- These behaviors are inappropriate because of the following:
  - The age difference between you and the students. You are an adult, and these students are adolescents in the developing stage of their lives. They are impressionable and still mentally developing.
  - The fact that some of the students may have disabilities that prevent them from understanding the nature of your comments.
  - The fact that these students may get teased about their disabilities in other settings; you can hurt their feelings and self-esteem through your comments.

- You are directed to immediately stop the following:
  - Making inappropriate comments to students
  - Making fun of students
  - Making sarcastic comments about students

If the inappropriate behavior does not stop immediately, further disciplinary action can occur, up to and including termination of employment.

I understand and agree to the terms of this plan.

_____   _____

Employee signature   Supervisor signature

DELIVERING A PERFORMANCE CONCERN OR TERMINATION MESSAGE TO A PARAPROFESSIONAL OR TEACHING ASSISTANT

As in previous chapters, we now provide an outline for a conference you could deliver to a teaching assistant or paraprofessional in order to communicate your concerns about marginal or deficient behaviors (see Figure 7.3). We have kept the basic conference format the same for all employee groups so that you can learn one template. Once you understand the template, you can add to it based on the employee and the situation.

Figure 7.3	Template for Delivering a Performance Concern or Termination Message to a Paraprofessional or Teaching Assistant

Set a professional tone

In this phase of the conference, the supervisor opens the conference and lets the paraprofessional know that it will be a professional experience. *Example statement: Thank you for meeting with me. I need to talk to you about a concern I have.*

(Your planned opening here)

_____

_____

_____

_____

_____

Provide an overview of the conferencing process

People like it when they know what is coming up. Use this phase of the conference to lay out the plan for your time with the paraprofessional. *Example statement: During this conference, I'll share my concerns related to your performance and give you specific examples of what I mean.*

(Your planned overview here)

_____

_____

_____

_____

_____

Define deficient performance areas

In this phase of the conference, clearly define what is deficient about the paraprofessional's overall performance and why it is deficient. *Example statement: I have a concern about how you relate to students. In class, when they ask you questions, you*

Figure 7.3 (Continued)

snap at them. You look bothered and annoyed when they need your help. Next, I'll give you more information about your specific performance in these areas.

(Your discussion of deficiencies here)

_____

_____

_____

_____

_____

Give clear, clean examples of deficiency

Be sure to provide clear examples from the observations and other data courses where the deficiency or deficiencies are occurring. *Example statement: On March 14, I overheard you lecturing a student for asking a question. On March 15, I heard you raise your voice when another student seemed to not understand your response. Finally, on April 11, you told a student to return to his desk because he was bothering you and needed to figure things out for himself. You have continued this behavior in spite of us talking about the need to stop this behavior on at least five separate occasions.*

(Your examples here)

_____

_____

_____

_____

_____

Restate why this behavior is an issue and that the performance is not meeting school standards

At this point you may think that what you have covered is very clear, but you need to sum up all of the information you just presented and remind the employee that he or she is not meeting standards. You need to let the employee know if the behavior does not improve you will be recommending termination. *First example statement (which is used if you are going to develop a growth plan): When you treat students in this manner, it sets a bad tone for their learning and upsets them, and they become harder to deal with later. It sets a bad tone or reputation for our school. If this behavior cannot be addressed, I may need to move to terminate your employment, but I'm sure we can work things out. Second example statement (which is used if you are going to move to termination): Since this behavior is detrimental to your students and you have refused to stop doing it after repeated reminders, I am terminating your employment here in this building.*

(Your conclusions here)

_____

_____

_____

_____

_____

Share strategies for improvement and outline your follow-up plan for supporting the employee

Talk to the paraprofessional about what he or she can do to respond to the evaluation, the next steps in the process, and any other rights he or she has in relation to the evaluation. *Example statement: Here is what you need to do in order to change your behavior (share specific plan and strategies). I will check in with you in a few days to see how you are doing. It is my expectation that your efforts should be able to address my concerns.*

(Your strategies and plan here)

_____

_____

_____

_____

_____

AN EXAMPLE OF A MEETING AND LETTER
OF REPRIMAND FOR A PARAPROFESSIONAL

The following is an example of an incident involving a paraprofessional falsifying a time sheet, followed by a letter of reprimand/notification for the paraprofessional.

❖

Ken, an elementary school principal, had a concern about one of his paraprofessionals who was using a lot of sick days. Ken learned from another employee that the paraprofessional was not sick and was thus falsifying time sheets to use the time to attend various events in the community. Ken thought it would be best to seek assistance from the Human Resource Department, which decided to do an investigation and to inform the paraprofessional that the department would be doing so.

Here is an example of a letter notifying the paraprofessional about the impending investigation.

Date

Re: Use of Sick Leave

Dear (employee's name)

This letter is to notify you that you are the subject of an investigation by (name of the school district). Please contact the director of human resources for a meeting. You have the right to have a union representative present. You have the right to refuse to answer any questions. This will be your only opportunity to provide the district with information concerning the allegations against you. If you do not provide any information, the district will rely on the information it has already collected.

The specific allegations against you are that you falsified a time sheet. Concerns about your absenteeism and your use of sick leave may be addressed.

Failure to contact the district in this matter will result in the investigation concluding without your input. Please contact me by (date).

Sincerely,

Principal

❖

SUMMARY

Paraprofessionals and teaching assistants play an important role in the success of students. As a school leader, it's crucial that you are able to work with marginal and deficient paraprofessionals. In this chapter, we have provided tools and templates to assist you in this task. As you think about the content of this chapter, reflect on the following:

- What are some of the unique characteristics of paraprofessionals that you need to take into consideration when working with them?
- What are the steps that you should include in a conference designed to inform a paraprofessional of a deficient performance?
- How could you put together a deficiency letter to inform a paraprofessional of your concern with her performance?

In Chapter 8, you will learn the unique characteristics of custodians and how to deal with them if they become marginal or deficient. Some of the techniques used with other employee groups also work well with custodians, but you will also learn about specialized ideas for working with these staff members.

NOTES

Write any notes that you think might be helpful to you as you implement the strategies/ideas presented in this chapter with your difficult employees. Feel free to refer back to these notes as you need to when confronting their issues or behaviors.

_____

_____

_____

_____

_____

_____

_____

_____

_____

_____

_____

_____

_____

_____

_____

_____

_____

_____

8

Strategies for Working With Difficult/Marginal Custodians

Even though these staff members do most of their work behind the normal limelight of the school, their contributions to the success of the teachers and students cannot be underestimated. When your custodial staff members are on track and working together, your school is extremely clean and safe; when this group or a member of it is not working effectively, the entire building suffers. In most cases, the internal drive and customer service orientation of custodians helps them work hard independently to ensure the proper operation of the school. In some cases, however, you will need to address concerns about them and either help them improve their performance or work to terminate their services. In this chapter, you will learn about the following:

- identifying the potential difficult behaviors you may face with custodians
- clearly communicating to custodians your expectations for performance and customer interaction
- developing improvement plans for deficient custodians
- delivering improvement conferences to staff members who are not meeting expectations

POSSIBLE DIFFICULT CUSTODIAL BEHAVIOR

Over the years, in our own experiences and in our work with principals, we have seen a variety of difficult behaviors exhibited by custodians. Here are some of the typical issues faced by principals.

- *Too much work:* This is the type of person who thinks the workload is unfair and that he is doing most of it at your school.

Strategies for working with this type of custodian. This person will have a hard time seeing that things are fair. Talk with him and show him how the job assignments were delegated. If you think the job assignments are fair, you may need to just tell him that and ignore his complaints.

- *Disloyal employee:* A disloyal employee can talk positively to your face but negatively when you are not around.

Strategies for working with this type of custodian. At times, other staff members will tell you when they experience this type of behavior. Be careful in confronting this type of situation without considering the potential impact on the person who tipped you off. If you confront the backstabber without naming the source of your information, she will deny the accusation, but you will still have raised her awareness of the situation. Monitor her behavior, and adjust accordingly.

- *Constant negative behavior:* Obviously, someone who exhibits a negative attitude is not pleasant to be around and can set the tone in a department or building. He looks at everything from the negative side. Whenever you talk with him, he brings up every objection possible.

Strategies for working with this type of custodian. Consider taking this person aside and telling him about his negativity and its impact on the rest of the school. When you are holding this conversation, provide clear and specific examples. Be sure you consider the impact of this person sharing the content of your conversation with others and painting you in a negative light.

- *Opposition to your supervision:* This custodian will usually take a strong stand against you on almost any issue. She is not shy about confronting you privately or in the presence of others.

Strategies for working with this type of custodian. Consider sitting down with her and laying your cards on the table to find out why the relationship is negative. You may want to have a witness in the room with you when you conduct this conference. If you can develop some type of agreement to improve your relationship, you may be able to work things out. If not, one of you may need to go.

• *Short temper:* A custodian with a short temper can be extremely difficult to work with. Little things can set him off, and he can get angry and unreasonable.

Strategies for working with this type of custodian. Because of the unpredictable and volatile nature of this type of custodian, he needs to be approached and the behavior immediately placed under control. If you choose to meet with a person with a short temper, be sure to have a witness with you and select a calm, open place in which to hold this meeting. Back up your assertions and concerns with factual information and data. Watch the person carefully for signs that he may be getting upset. Temporarily back away from the confrontation using reflecting or paraphrasing skills.

• *Inefficient worker:* You may encounter a custodian who is extremely slow in completing her work. This not only wastes time but also can cause poor morale among the other workers. It needs to be addressed.

Strategies for working with this type of custodian. If a custodian is new to a school or a job assignment, it is reasonable that she may be slower than others because she is still learning the job expectations. After a reasonable amount of transition time has passed, you should be able to expect this person to complete her assigned area in a timely manner. If this does not happen, you may need to watch her work, monitor her job schedule, and spend time problem solving this situation. In the end, you may need to look at terminating her because of slow task completion.

EFFECTIVE DELEGATION OF TASKS AND ASSIGNMENTS

In working with difficult/marginal custodians, it is important to be specific and clear in delegating tasks. If you are clear and specific you can follow up more effectively than if you are vague and less specific. Let's see how Dawn, a high school principal, uses this strategy to work with Larry, her head custodian:

In getting the school ready for prom, Dawn wants several things in place. She meets with Larry to outline her wishes for the event. She lays out a list for him that includes all of the cleaning and room arrangements that need to be taken care of before the upcoming event. She asks Larry to make sure these things are completed by noon on the Friday before prom. Dawn sets up a time to meet with Larry so they can go over the checklist and he can inform her of what has been done and any outstanding issues that need to be addressed before the event. Dawn has shared with Larry both her general expectations for the event and the exact details pertaining to the work he needs to do. Because she has effectively delegated the tasks to Larry, he is able to complete them on his own but he also knows that Dawn is there to help if he has any questions. The planning and preparation for the event work well.

Since Dawn has effectively delegated the tasks for prom preparation, Larry has a road map to follow. He is not a difficult custodian to work with, but this strategy also works well for difficult/deficient employees for the following reasons:

- The communication between the supervisor and employee is clear and direct.
- By effectively delegating tasks, the supervisor provides a clear picture for the expectations of the completed tasks but leaves responsibility for their implementation to the employee.
- Since the expectations are clear but the actual implementation is up to the custodian, the principal does not have to micromanage him in order to get the job done.
- Both the custodian and the supervisor have a clear picture for the finished job; the expectations for the job are set at the beginning to allow for a fair evaluation at the end.

Effective delegation of tasks is a good way to work with difficult/marginal custodians. But it takes some planning on your part in order to make sure that your delegation helps these employees stay focused. Use the template in Figure 8.1 to plan your delegation strategy.

To help you as you begin to use this process, a sample of a completed template is provided in Figure 8.2.

BASE AND SURFACE COMPETENCIES

In Chapter 2, we introduced a template to help you identify base and surface competencies (see Figure 2.1 for the blank reproducible template). Figure 8.3 is a sample of a completed template. It is important to familiarize yourself with these competencies because you need to assess whether any deficit skills relate to them. As was discussed in Chapter 2, base competency deficits are much more difficult to remediate than surface competency deficits. Each type of deficit also takes a slightly different set of plans and strategies to address in an employee.

| Figure 8.1 | Delegation Planning Template |

Delegation Step	Specific Text for Delegation Conference
1. Carefully think through the entire assignment, identifying the steps or subtasks that may need to be accomplished for it to be completed successfully.	
2. Think about the custodian to whom you are delegating the task. Identify his or her strengths; identify the challenges he or she typically faces when doing this sort of job. Think through specifically how you will need to communicate your expectations to this person.	
3. Talk with the person to whom you are delegating the task. Be sure to share why he or she is getting the task and any unique strengths you see as beneficial to the success of the project.	
4. Provide your vision for the completed task. The employee should be able to see what you want done with the assignment. Include your standards and timeline for the task.	
5. Ask the person to whom you are delegating this task to use his or her own words to describe what is desired for the final product. Have the custodian describe his or her picture of the completed task.	
6. Talk with the person and make sure you explain any needed skills or competencies that he or she will need in order to be successful.	
7. Determine a formal communication and assessment schedule at the beginning of the project.	
8. Provide positive feedback on the implementation efforts.	

Figure 8.2	Sample Completed Delegation Planning Template

Delegation Step	Specific Text for Delegation Conference
1. Carefully think through the entire assignment, identifying the steps or subtasks that may need to be accomplished for it to be completed successfully.	Components needed for a clean front entrance to the school: • The front doors are clean and freshly painted. • Trash and garbage are removed. • The sidewalk leading to the front door is clear of trash and sand/dirt. • The windows in the doors are free of dirt and fingerprints. • The mats in the foyer are clean and neatly arranged.
2. Think about the custodian to whom you are delegating the task. Identify his or her strengths; identify the challenges he or she typically faces when doing this sort of job. Think through specifically how you will need to communicate your expectations to this person.	Joan will be doing this job. She can have a hard time seeing areas that are not neat and clean. We will have to brainstorm how she can see and address the areas of concern.
3. Talk with the person to whom you are delegating the task. Be sure to share why he or she is getting the task and any unique strengths you see as beneficial to the success of the project.	I'll set up a meeting with Joan to talk about the front entrance job and to let her know why I chose her for the assignment.
4. Provide your vision for the completed task. The employee should be able to see what you want done with the assignment. Include your standards and timeline for the task.	When the project is completed, it should • be clear of weeds and trash, • have plants and flowers that are balanced in height and density, • stay clean and clear of trash, and • continue to be trimmed.
5. Ask the person to whom you are delegating this task to use his or her own words to describe what is desired for the final product. Have the custodian describe his or her picture of the completed task.	I'll ask Joan to share what she will be doing and to describe the level of cleanliness desired for the front entrance.
6. Talk with the person and make sure you explain any needed skills or competencies that he or she will need in order to be successful.	I'll ask Joan to share what might be most helpful to her. I will teach/explain what needs to be done.

(Continued)

Figure 8.2 (Continued)

Delegation Step	Specific Text for Delegation Conference
7. Determine a formal communication and assessment schedule at the beginning of the project.	Joan and I will meet on a monthly basis to check in and see how the front entrance is shaping up.
8. Provide positive feedback on the implementation efforts.	I'll make it a point to enter the building from the front entrance at least once a week. I'll find Joan and write her at least two notes thanking her for her efforts.

Figure 8.3 Sample Completed Base and Surface Competencies Template for Custodians

Name Ellen Smith   Job or Position Head Custodian

Job Requirement/ Competency	Base Competency	Surface Competency	Deficit Skill
Ability to anticipate needed priorities and upcoming tasks	X		
Understanding of the various cleaning products and their application in the building		X	
Ability to build rapport and a sense of team among the custodians in the building	X		
Ability to listen to and use constructive criticism	X		
Ability to develop and adjust the work schedules of the custodial team members as needed		X	
Ability to listen to and calm down an angry person when he or she encounters a problem	X		

GROWTH PLANS

As you think about addressing your concerns for employee performance issues, it is a good idea to develop a written plan, which helps to reinforce the severity of the problem and provides documentation to be used in tracking the performance and the interventions attempted. Figure 8.4 is a sample of a completed growth plan to help you get an idea of how one might be developed for an employee. (See Figure 5.2 for the blank reproducible version of the template.).

Figure 8.4 Sample Completed Growth Plan for Custodians

(INSERT SCHOOL NAME)
EMPLOYEE GROWTH PLAN

You are receiving this growth plan because serious concerns exist about your performance here at (insert school name). These concerns are summarized below:

- Your inability to adequately maintain the cleanliness of your assigned areas. Some examples of this problem include:
  - You repeatedly leave chairs and desks in disarray in your assigned classrooms.
  - When you vacuum the rooms, you just do the center; you fail to move furniture around to clean the entire room. Paper scraps are left along the edges for several days at a time.
  - You fail to clean marker boards in the classrooms. This leaves a dull appearance on these boards.
  - You fail to empty your trash on a consistent basis.

- To address this situation, both your immediate supervisor, Jake Smith, and I have talked to you on the following dates:
  - On January 17, Mr. Smith met with you and identified these concerns. You said you would be more careful and do a better job in the future.
  - On February 1, because the problem persisted, Mr. Smith asked me to join in on a meeting with you to address the issues. At that meeting, we worked out a verbal plan for you to address these issues.
  - On February 10, we met again to talk about the situation. While there was some improvement, your work was still below acceptable standards.

(Continued)

Figure 8.4 (Continued)

- We are addressing these cleanliness issues for the following reasons:
  - ○ The lack of cleanliness causes a potential safety issue for the students. The objects left on the floor could cause someone to trip and fall.
  - ○ The lack of cleanliness makes the school look bad and detracts from the positive culture we are trying to establish here.
  - ○ All of the other custodians are able to keep their areas clean; your lack of cleanliness detracts from the work the others in this department do.

- You are directed to immediately do the following:
  - ○ Completely clean your rooms to the standards of the building. We have shown you the level of cleanliness we expect on a daily basis.
  - ○ Move all furniture in order to completely vacuum the rooms. When you are finished cleaning, move the furniture back to the original prescribed room arrangement unless directed to do otherwise by the teachers, your direct supervisor, or the administration.
  - ○ Check in with your immediate supervisor on a weekly basis to get feedback about your cleaning efforts.

If the cleanliness of the rooms does not markedly improve immediately, you could face more severe consequences up to and including termination of employment.

I understand and agree to the terms of this plan.

_____   _____

Employee signature   Supervisor signature

DELIVERING A PERFORMANCE OR SKILL DEFICIT CONCERN TO A CUSTODIAL EMPLOYEE

Even with your best efforts to provide clear direction and support in helping your employees be successful, you will run into times when you need to confront a custodian about work performance. The template in Figure 8.5 is provided to give you some guidelines in delivering a growth conference. We have used a similar template for each school employee group so that you can become familiar with a common format. Once you know the format, adjustments can be made based on the unique group or situation you face.

Figure 8.5	Template for Delivering a Performance or Skill Deficit Concern to a Custodial Employee

Set a professional tone

In this phase of the conference, the supervisor opens the conference and lets the custodian know that it will be a professional experience. *Example statement: Thank you for meeting with me. I need to talk to you about a concern I have.*

(Your planned opening here)

_____

_____

_____

_____

_____

Provide an overview of the conferencing process

People like it when they know what is coming up. Use this phase of the conference to lay out the plan for your time with the custodian. *Example statement: During this conference, I'll share my concerns related to your performance and give you specific examples of what I mean.*

(Your planned overview here)

_____

_____

_____

_____

_____

Define deficient performance areas

In this phase of the conference, clearly define what is deficient about the custodian's overall performance and why it is deficient. *Example statement: I have a concern*

(Continued)

Figure 8.5   (Continued)

about how you relate to the night guests we have that rent our gyms. When they ask you questions or want you to set up a piece of equipment for them, you snap at them. You look bothered and annoyed when they need your help. Next, I'll give you more information about your specific performance in these areas.

(Your discussion of deficiencies here)

_____

_____

_____

_____

_____

Give clear, clean examples of deficiency

Be sure to provide clear examples from the observations and other data courses where the deficiency or deficiencies are occurring. *Example statement: On September 15, I saw you get mad at a party because they wanted the basketball hoops lowered. On October 21, the leader of the Boy Scouts that meet in the gym reported to me that you lectured them because you had to set up tables for them. You told them they should have called in advance. On January 19, you raised your voice when the PTO president asked you to get the coffee pot set up for the meeting. You have continued this behavior in spite of us talking about the need to stop this behavior on at least five occasions.*

(Your examples here)

_____

_____

_____

_____

_____

Restate why this behavior is an issue and that the performance is not meeting the school standards

At this point you may think that what you have covered is very clear, but you need to sum up all of the information you just presented and remind the employee that he or she is not meeting standards. You need to let the employee know that if the behavior does not improve you will be recommending termination. *Example statement: When you treat people in this manner, it upsets them and hurts our public image. It also makes them harder to deal with later. It sets a bad tone or reputation for our school. If this behavior cannot be addressed, I may need to move to terminate your employment, but I'm sure we can work things out.*

(Your conclusions here)

_____

_____

_____

_____

_____

Share strategies for improvement and outline your follow-up plan for supporting the employee

Talk to the custodian about what he or she can do to respond to the evaluation, the next steps in the process, and any other rights he or she has in relation to the evaluation. *Example statement: Here is what you need to do in order to change your behavior (share specific plan and strategies). I will check in with you in a few days to see how you are doing. It is my expectation that your efforts should be able to address my concerns.*

(Insert your own language here)

_____

_____

_____

_____

_____

SUMMARY

In this chapter, we have discussed strategies for dealing with difficult custodians. Thankfully, most of our employees are focused and interested in doing a good job and getting along well with others. Normally, only a small percentage of employees make it their mission to be difficult in the workplace. As the school principal, you do not have to put up with this kind of behavior and you can begin to address the situation so that these difficult employees do not make life miserable for all of the other people who are interested in doing a good job in your school.

As you think back to some of the major things that you learned as a result of reading this chapter, take a few minutes to reflect on the following questions:

- What are some of the major behaviors that difficult people engage in, and how can you deal with these behaviors?
- How can you, as immediate supervisor of some of these difficult people, deal with their problems without taking on their issues?
- What kinds of strategies can you employ to protect your emotional safety as you confront difficult people?

Your custodians are key to your success as a school leader. The ideas and strategies outlined in this chapter and the information provided in the other chapters of this book will help you as you work to improve their performance and address the issues they bring to the workplace.

NOTES

Write any notes that you think might be helpful to you as you implement the strategies/ideas presented in this chapter with your difficult employees. Feel free to refer back to these notes as you need to when confronting their issues or behaviors.

_____

_____

_____

_____

_____

_____

_____

_____

_____

_____

_____

_____

_____

_____

References

Eller, J. (2004). *Effective group facilitation in education: How to energize meetings and manage difficult groups.* Thousand Oaks, CA: Corwin.

Eller, J., & Eller, S. (2009). *Creative strategies to improve school culture.* Thousand Oaks, CA: Corwin.

Kuhn, T. S. (1996). *The structure of scientific revolutions* (3rd ed.). Chicago: University of Chicago Press.

Index

CORWIN
A SAGE Company

The Corwin logo—a raven striding across an open book—represents the union of courage and learning. Corwin is committed to improving education for all learners by publishing books and other professional development resources for those serving the field of PreK–12 education. By providing practical, hands-on materials, Corwin continues to carry out the promise of its motto: **"Helping Educators Do Their Work Better."**